NURTURING CREATIVITY IN THE CLASSROOM

An exploration of consensus across theory and practice

To order, or for details of our bulk discounts, please go to our website www.criticalpublishing. com or contact our distributor, Ingram Publisher Services (IPS UK), 10 Thornbury Road, Plymouth PL6 7PP, telephone 01752 202301 or email IPSUK.orders@ingramcontent.com.

CRITICAL
PUBLISHING

NURTURING CREATIVITY IN THE CLASSROOM

An exploration of consensus across theory and practice

Karen Hosack Janes

First published in 2022 by Critical Publishing Ltd

British Library Cataloguing in Publication Data
A CIP record for this book is available from the British Library

ISBN: 9781913453893

This book is also available in the following e-book formats:

EPUB ISBN: 9781913453916
Adobe e-book ISBN: 9781913453923

Cover design by Out of House Limited
Text design by Out of House Limited
Project Management by Deanta Global Publishing Services, Dublin, Ireland
Typeset by Deanta Global Publishing Services, Chennai, India
Printed and bound in Great Britain by 4edge, Essex

Critical Publishing
3 Connaught Road
St Albans
AL3 5RX

www.criticalpublishing.com

Paper from responsible sources

Contents

Acknowledgements

Many thanks to the creative people who so generously shared their experiences with me when I was writing this book. I am especially grateful to Bob and Roberta Smith, Marcus du Sautoy, Toby Thompson, Julian Nott, Alex Duarte-Davies, Sophie Jacobs-Wyburn and Yasmin Sidhwa. Our conversations were personal highlights of mine during the strange times of the pandemic.

Throughout my life I have been fortunate to be surrounded by nurturing, creative people. Therefore, I would like to extend my gratitude and love to all my family, friends and colleagues who have made valuing the arts and playing with ideas an everyday collaborative reality for me.

Quoted material on pages 98 and 99 is used with the kind permission of Complicité.

Dedication

For Lawrence,
whose creativity brings huge joy

About the author

Karen Hosack Janes

Karen Hosack Janes is a lecturer at Oxford Brookes University and an education consultant, specialising in pedagogy that nurtures creative development. She has worked at a senior level in the education and museums and galleries sectors, and now supports teachers and teacher training students in designing activities that maximise learners' creative agency. Formerly head of schools at the National Gallery, London, she has run education programmes and visited numerous schools across the UK, enabling her to see first-hand how creativity is taught and the challenges teachers encounter. This book contains a wealth of practical advice, from Karen and many others, to help in the development of your own and your pupils' personal creativity.

Introduction

Why creativity is difficult to define, and why it's important to try

Do you consider yourself to be creative? Whether you do or not, to answer the question you will need to have a perception of what being creative means. Do you, for example, associate it with certain activities or particular subject areas? If so, which? Do you think being creative is something positive or negative?

If you are a teacher, like me, you might find the last question a little strange because, as educators, we are regularly told that creativity is a *'good thing'* (Coate and Boulos, 2012, p 129). Indeed, the national curriculum for England (DfE, 2014) aims to *'engender an appreciation of human creativity and achievement'* (p 6). However, agreement on what creativity looks like in the classroom is contested. For instance, a study looking at teachers' perceptions of creativity (Kettler et al, 2018) found that behaviours such as *'taking chances'* or being *'impulsive'* and *'autonomous'* were thought by some teachers to be *'undesirable'* (p 167). Yet, opportunities encouraging these behaviours, like giving pupils the freedom to take risks and to have the space and time to explore and experiment with ideas, are recognised by many to be essential for imaginations to open and innovation to take place (for example, Boden, 1990; Craft, 2000; NACCCE, 1999).

Perhaps being creative, and enabling creativity to flourish, therefore, is to do with our personal perspective on what it means to learn and to teach. An apprentice model prevalent in many professions, including the arts, where the apprentice perfects their own skills by copying the techniques and style of a master craftsperson – such as in the artisan workshops of Western Europe dating back before the Renaissance, or in the creative traditions of China and Japan – is some people's idea of a creative education. For others, a more expressive and freer environment is thought to be conducive to developing creative skills. Or, depending on what is being taught, somewhere in-between these two descriptions is believed by others to provide the most effective conditions for nurturing creativity.

Finding a common language for creativity

So, clarifying what creativity looks like is tricky, which makes finding a common language to talk about it difficult. Its complex nature means that the word 'creative' can be referred to as a noun, where it can take the form of creative products, or as a verb in terms of cause, effect and interaction, also as a cluster of psychological factors within individual people, or as a congenial environment in which a degree of risk-taking may be tolerated (Cropley, 2001). When the Cambridge Primary Review (an enquiry into the English education system in 2010) put out a call for views on educational practice, submissions from individuals and organisations included the word 'creativity' to refer to *'individual qualities, aims, processes or outcomes'*. The final report comments that *'creativity ... appeared to mean taking risks or just doing things differently'* and *'referred variously to the child's creativity, teacher creativity and the "creative" subjects like art, music or drama'* (Alexander, 2010, p 226).

The absence of a commonly held idea about what creativity looks like is similarly demonstrated in a national schools' survey undertaken by Arts Council England (ACE, 2020) at the start of the global coronavirus pandemic. In order *'to gather indicative information from schools about the potential needs and creative aspirations for their pupils from autumn 2020 onwards'* (p 2) teachers were asked to rank from a list of six approaches to home learning which they thought *'worked best during Lockdown'* (p 4). The list included: *'Creative activities'*, *'project-based activities'*, *'research/ enquiry-based activities'*, *'challenge-based activities'*, *'normal timetable delivered virtually'* and *'revision based activities'*. However, by presenting the approaches as distinct from one another, the impression given is that *'project-based'*, *'research/ enquiry-based'* and *'challenge-based'* activities are to be considered discrete activities, and also that these are not *'creative activities'*. The separation implies no overlap. Perhaps, in this case, the term *'creative activities'* is intended to refer to 'creative' subjects like art, music and drama, as mentioned in the *Cambridge Primary Review*? If so, this could be considered a narrow view of creativity endorsed by Arts Council England.

Creativity as a single concept

A definition that attempts to comprehend creativity as a single concept was developed in 1999 in the UK by the National Advisory Committee on Creative and Cultural Education (NACCCE):

> *Imaginative activity fashioned so as to produce outcomes that are both original and of value.*

> (NACCCE, 1999, p 30)

The committee was set up by the UK government:

> *To make recommendations to the Secretaries of State on the creative and cultural development of young people through formal and informal education: to take stock of current provision and to make proposals for principles, policies and practice.*
>
> (p 2)

The findings of the commission were published in a report titled All Our Futures: Creativity, Culture and Education (NACCCE, 1999). Claims include that creativity promotes '*the freedom to innovate and take risks*' (p 10), that '*creativity always involves originality*' and that '*historic originality*' (which the report defines as work that is original in terms of anyone's previous output in a particular field) is '*more likely to emerge from a system which encourages the creative capacities of everyone*' (p 32). Although the enquiry had an arts focus, the report emphasises that dichotomies between curriculum subjects are unhelpful, and that '*creative and cultural education are not just subjects in the curriculum, they are the general function of education*' (p 6). In the US, a corresponding commission with similar conclusions was conducted by the President's Committee on the Arts and the Humanities (PCAH, 2011). This report was published under the title Reinvesting in Arts Education: Winning America's Future through Creative Schools. Recommendations from both the UK and US commissions led to substantial funding being made available to arts education initiatives at the beginning of the millennium; a level of funding that has since continued to fall.

The NACCCE definition of creativity has been cited in the rationales of a wide number of UK government initiatives, policies and reports (for example, CCE, 2007, 2009, 2012; DfES, 2003; MLA, 2005; Ofsted, 2010; QCA, 2004). One of these includes guidance notes for teachers published by the Qualifications and Curriculum Authority (QCA) titled Creativity: Find It, Promote It (2004). The NACCCE definition is acknowledged and echoed in the publication by the labelling of the '*Characteristics of creativity*' as '*Imagination and purpose*', '*Originality*' and '*Value*' (p 7). The resource goes on to state that '*creativity improves pupils' self-esteem, motivation and achievement*' by making pupils

> *more interested in discovering things for themselves; more open to new ideas; keen to work with others; and willing to work beyond lesson time when pursuing an idea or vision.*
>
> (p 9)

It asserts that teachers are

> *likely to see pupils being creative if they see them questioning and challenging; making connections and seeking relationships; envisioning what might be; exploring ideas; and reflecting critically on ideas, actions and outcomes.*
>
> (p 10)

But, despite the fact that there is obvious merit in trying to summarise creativity as a generic single concept, there has been some criticism about 'creative skills' being a '*catch-all*' expression (Sefton-Green et al, 2011, p 2) and '*something of a cliché*' (Alexander, 2010, p 226). Coupled with this, the positive impact of creativity advocated in these, and similar, documents tend not to be supported with high-quality empirical evidence. Let us look at this issue now.

Research into creativity

There is a difference between measuring and assessing educational impact. Measurement is to do with descriptions of quantity, with things being measured against something else. Assessment is to do with appraising the value of something, sometimes of something that has been measured (Eisner, 2002). Common problems when attempting to measure creativity include establishing specific objectives to evaluate. This is especially tricky for qualities that might be elusive, or for evaluating objectives that evolve over time, or for outcomes that are unexpected. Because of this, quantitative methodologies making causal links between creativity and subjects easier to test (such as those scored in standardised tests) are often adopted by researchers looking to 'prove' the impact of 'creative' activities. But this approach is even knottier. For example, the academic attainment results of young people known to have attended workshops run as part of the Creative Partnerships programme (a UK government scheme from 2002 to 2011) were compared to similar young people nationally that did not attend a Creative Partnership project (Durbin et al, 2010; Kendall, 2008). The methodology, however, is problematic for several reasons. First, the Creative Partnerships projects tended to be short-term, and therefore isolating the impact of sometimes one-off experiences on test results from other influential factors is impossible. Second, as pointed out by Sefton-Green (2007) in a think piece considering evidence gathered by the Creative Partnerships programme, the methodology does not reflect the primary aim of the programme: '*to foster creativity in schools with a view to creating long-term structural change across the education system as a whole*' (ACE, 2007, p 3). And finally, the design of the research does not enable an analysis of the experiences of the participants. Consequently, the data has very limited value for informing further projects and advancing an understanding of the nature of creativity. In any case, the findings of these studies showed very little difference between the two groups.

Two large international meta-analyses examining data across a wide number of arts education studies found no causal links could be claimed between arts education and standardised test results (including specially devised tests) (Winner and Hetland, 2000; See and Kokotsaki, 2017). Another meta-analysis, this time looking at the relationship between creative self-efficacy and different creativity measurements (Haase et al, 2018), found little agreement on what creativity is beyond aspects of '*novelty and usefulness*' (p 2), concluding this leads to inconsistencies when attempting to measure creativity. Similarly, a meta-analysis examining 35 research papers on creativity in education (Cremin and Chappell, 2019) concludes there is '*a lack of coherent research into what creative pedagogies are and what they do*' (p 3). Nevertheless, the authors of this study uncover in their analysis what they describe as '*seven interrelating features of creative pedagogy*':

'Risk-taking', 'encouraging autonomy and agency', 'generating and exploring ideas', 'playfulness', 'problem-solving', 'co-constructing and collaborating' and 'teacher creativity' (p 13). Although what is meant by some of these terms is not always defined in the papers examined, and inconsistencies in definitions are apparent, these words and phrases, like others used to describe creative behaviours previously referred to in this introduction, while not evidence of impact are nonetheless helpful in pinpointing what conditions are generally considered important for creativity to flourish. This book assists in unpicking some of these words and phrases and adds to the conversation about which conditions are effective in nurturing creative development by gathering viewpoints across theory and practice and trying to find consensus.

Teaching for creativity

In the UK, 20 years after the publication of the NACCCE (1999) report All Our Futures: Creativity, Culture and Education (as previously mentioned), another large UK enquiry was undertaken into creativity and education, known as the Durham Commission (2019). The report, which is a collaboration between Durham University and Arts Council England, clarifies what the commission perceives as 'creativity' and 'creative thinking'. Both definitions include an expectation for originality, consistent with the NACCCE definition of creativity. In addition, the Durham Commission defines 'teaching for creativity':

> Creativity: The capacity to imagine, conceive, express, or make something that was not there before.

> Creative thinking: A process through which knowledge, intuition and skills are applied to imagine, express or make something novel or individual in its contexts. Creative thinking is present in all areas of life. It may appear spontaneous, but it can be underpinned by perseverance, experimentation, critical thinking and collaboration.

> Teaching for creativity: Explicitly using pedagogies and practices that cultivate creativity in young people.

> (Durham Commission, 2019, p 96)

The definition of 'teaching for creativity' is provided to distinguish between:

- a teacher teaching in what could be described as a novel, engaging way; and

- a teacher who is specifically aiming to nurture the individual creative development of pupils.

A clear distinction between these two is crucial because it is not necessarily the case that a teacher teaching in a creative manner, using their own creative skills, leads to pupils individually developing their own creativity. We will discuss this point at length throughout this book as we explore consensus around creativity and how to nurture it. But, before we continue along that road, let us take a look for a moment at why it is an important one to go on.

Why are creative skills important?

During the Covid-19 pandemic the need for education to equip young people for the world of work that they will become part of was brought into sharp focus. The World Economic Forum (an international non-governmental organisation) reported in 2020 that the Covid-19 recession and an accelerated increase in automation created a *'double-disruption'* (WEF, 2020a, p 5) for workers, necessitating innovative ways to think about the future. They predict that by 2025 a shift in the balance of tasks done by machines at work, as opposed to being done by humans, will mean globally 85 million jobs being displaced. Reassuringly, however, simultaneously it has been modelled that '97 *million new roles may emerge that are more adapted to the new division of labour'* (p 5).

An analysis of occupations considered to be resistant to automation was conducted by the University of Oxford and the UK-based policy and research foundation Nesta in 2015 (Bakhshi et al, 2015). The findings show that the most likely jobs to continue to be needed to be done by humans are those requiring working towards end goals, sometimes with others, that are not fully specified in advance. Published under the title *Creativity Vs Robots*, the report suggests professions considered more future-proof than others, include, for example, doctor, scientist, IT/media specialist, journalist, lawyer, designer, artist, novelist and (happily) teacher. The report tells us that machines *'struggle when tasks are highly interpretative'* (p 19), this is because computers find it hard to emulate natural human emotion.

Marcus du Sautoy, professor of mathematics at the University of Oxford, explains in his bestseller *The Creativity Code: How AI Is Learning to Write, Paint and Think* (2019) how algorithms are now being coded to 'learn' about human behaviour from the mountain of digital data we produce every day. This includes algorithms learning from their own failures. He tells us that it is a bottom-up process, rather than the top-down one that Ada Lovelace in the mid-nineteenth century believed analytical machines were only capable of, where you cannot get more out than you put in. As a result, nowadays algorithms are capable of being our serious opponents in strategy games like chess, thinking several moves ahead. They can drive cars in busy traffic, and pick out clothes, music and TV programmes that we might like. We sometimes even 'chat' to them when making online enquiries without always knowing we are conversing with a machine. Even so, according to Marcus du Sautoy, it is our innate capacity for compassion that stops algorithms managing to convincingly pass themselves off as human.

So, it seems that occupations and other human endeavours that require imagining what it is like to be someone else cannot (for now) be fully automated. But, to ensure that future generations have the skills with which to cope and indeed make the most of the transformations that mass computerisation will inevitably and increasingly bring to all of our lives, we need to harness the power of our children's imaginations.

Bakhshi et al (2015) say in *Creativity Vs Robots* that the jobs resistant to automation are the ones which require honed social and emotional skills, particularly in communication, persuasion, motivation and negotiation, as well as other skills needed to make non-routine decisions. They make the case for the role of the educator in this landscape to assist pupils in developing their own sense of individuality so they can think independently, including in collaboration with others. The World Economic Forum argues in an article on its website, titled 'Our education system is losing relevance: Here's how to unleash its potential' (2020b), that we need to update how we view education so we can compete with smart machines. It states, '*the definition of quality and success has to move beyond standardized test scores to more holistic measurements tied to life improvements and societal impact*'. A similar message was conveyed by an international audience at the WISE and Salzburg Global Seminar online conference *Education Disrupted* in April 2020 where debates focused on the future needs of children across the world. 1173 delegates answered a poll asking '*What should your schools and systems be putting in the center of their planning for rebuilding education?*' 75.6 per cent of respondents voted that the 'well-being of students and teachers' should be pivotal; 13.3 per cent chose 'the whole child' as centrally important; 10.6 per cent voted for 'curriculum'; with just 0.5 per cent voting for 'testing'.

This book considers whether an education (in and out of the classroom) that focuses on nurturing creative skills (understood as those where there is an expectation for originality and independent thought) would provide children with the quality of education that could serve them well and span their lifetimes. For this reason, the next chapter gathers the thoughts of professional people well-known for their creativity to gain insight into what they believe encourages creative development.

REFLECTIVE POINTS

- Do you consider yourself to be creative?
- Do you associate creativity with certain activities or particular subject areas?
- Do you think is it possible to define creativity as a single concept, or is it many?
- Is framing creativity in terms of social and emotional skills useful?
- Do you think a school curriculum that focuses on nurturing the creativity of individuals would serve pupils well?

Further reading

Bakhshi, H, Frey, C and Osborne, M (2015) Creativity Vs. Robots: The Creative Economy and the Future of Employment. [online] Available at: https://media.nesta.org.uk/documents/creativity_vs._robots_wv.pdf (accessed 28 October 2021).

Du Sautoy, M (2019) *The Creativity Code: How AI is Learning to Write, Paint and Think*. London: 4th Estate.

References

Alexander, R (ed.) (2010) *Children, Their World, Their Education: Final Report and Recommendations of the Cambridge Primary Review*. London: Routledge.

Arts Council England (ACE) (2007) Creative Partnerships, Research Digest 2002–2006. [online] Available at: https://www.creativitycultureeducation.org/publication/this-much-we-know/ (accessed 28 October 2021).

Arts Council England (ACE) (2020) National Arts Creative and Cultural Education Survey: Research Findings Final Report July 2020. [online] Available at: https://curiousminds.org.uk/wp-content/uploads/2020/08/National-Schools-Survey-2020-Summary-of-Findings.pdf (accessed 28 October 2021).

Bakhshi, H, Frey, C and Osborne, M (2015) Creativity Vs. Robots: The Creative Economy and the Future of Employment. [online] Available at: https://media.nesta.org.uk/documents/creativity_vs._robots_wv.pdf (accessed 28 October 2021).

Boden, M (1990) *The Creative Mind: Myths and Mechanisms*. London: Weidenfeld and Nicolson.

Coate, K and Boulos, A (2012) Creativity in Education: Challenging the Assumptions. *London Review of Education* 10 (2): 129–32.

Craft, A (2000) *Creativity across the Primary Curriculum: Framing and Developing Practice*. London: Routledge.

Creativity Culture and Education (CCE) (2007) *Creative Partnerships: Approach and Impact. This Much We Know*. Newcastle: CCE & Arts Council England.

Creativity Culture and Education (CCE) (2009) *Creative Partnerships: Changing Young Lives*. Newcastle: CCE & Arts Council England.

Creativity Culture and Education (CCE) (2012) *Creative Partnerships: Changing Young Lives*. Newcastle: CCE & Arts Council England.

Cremin, T and Chappell, K (2019) Creative Pedagogies: A Systematic Review. *Research Papers in Education*. Taylor & Francis Online.

Cropley, A J (2001) *Creativity in Education and Learning*. Abingdon: Routledge.

Department for Education (DfE) (2014) *The National Curriculum in England: Framework for Key Stages 1–4*. London: HMSO. [online] Available at: https://www.gov.uk/government/publications/national-curriculum-in-england-framework-for-key-stages-1-to-4 (accessed 16 August 2021).

Department for Education and Skills (DfES) (2003) *Excellence and Enjoyment: A Strategy for Primary Schools*. [online] Available at https://webarchive.nationalarchives.gov.uk/20040722022638/http://www.dfes.gov.uk/primarydocument/ (accessed 28 October 2021).

Du Sautoy, M (2019) *The Creativity Code: How AI is Learning to Write, Paint and Think*. London: 4th Estate.

Durbin, B, et al (2010) *The Impact of Creative Partnerships on School Attainment and Attendance*. Slough: National Foundation for Educational Research.

Durham Commission (2019) Durham Commission on Creativity and Education. [online] Available at: https://www.dur.ac.uk/resources/creativitycommission/DurhamReport.pdf (accessed 28 October 2021).

Eisner, E (2002) *The Arts and the Creation of Mind*. New Haven and London: Yale University Press.

Haase, J, Hoff, E, Hanel, P and Innes-Ker, A (2018) A Meta-Analysis of the Relationship between Creative Self-Efficacy and Different Creativity Measurements. *Creativity Research Journal*, 30(1): Abingdon: Routledge.

Kendall, L (2008) *The Longer-Term Impact of Creative Partnerships on the Attainment of Young People, Results 2005/-6*. Slough: National Foundation for Educational Research.

Kettler, T, Lamb, K, Willerson, A and Mullet, D (2018) Teachers' Perceptions of Creativity in the Classroom. *Creativity Research Journal*, 30 (2): 164–71.

Museums Libraries and Archives Council (MLA) (2005) *Inspiring Learning for All Framework*. London: Arts Council England. [online] Available at: https://le.ac.uk/rcmg/research-archive/engaging-archives (accessed 28 October 2021).

National Advisory Committee on Creative and Cultural Education (NACCCE) (1999) All Our Futures: Creativity, Culture and Education. [online] Available at: http://sirkenrobinson.com/pdf/allourfutures.pdf (accessed 28 October 2021).

Ofsted (2010) Learning: Creative Approaches that Raise Standards. [online] Available at: https://webarchive.nationalarchives.gov.uk/20141116012722/http://www.ofsted.gov.uk/node/2405 (accessed 28 October 2021).

President's Committee on the Arts and the Humanities (PCAH) (2011) Reinvesting in Arts Education: Winning America's Future through Creative Schools. [online] Available at: https://files.eric.ed.gov/fulltext/ED522818.pdf (accessed 28 October 2021).

Qualifications and Curriculum Authority (QCA) (2004) Creativity: Find It, Promote It. [online] Available at: https://www.literacyshed.com/uploads/1/2/5/7/12572836/1847211003.pdf (accessed 28 October 2021).

See, B and Kokotsaki, D (2017) Impact of Arts Education on the Cognitive and Non-cognitive Outcomes of School-Aged Children: A Review of Evidence. Available at: https://educationendowmentfoundation.org.uk/public/files/Presentations/Publications/Arts_Education_Review.pdf (accessed 28 October 2021).

Sefton-Green, J (2007) Thinkpiece: The Challenge of Defining Impact. [online] Available at: http://old.creativitycultureeducation.org/wp-content/uploads/This-Much-We-Know-Thinkpiece.pdf (accessed 28 October 2021).

Sefton-Green, J, Thomson, P, Jones, K and Bresler, L (eds) (2011) *The Routledge International Handbook of Creative Learning*. Abingdon: Routledge.

Winner, E and Hetland, L (2000) The Arts and Academic Achievement: What the Evidence Shows. *The Journal of Aesthetic Education (Double Issue)*, 34 (3/4), Illinois: University of Illinois Press.

World Economic Forum (WEF) (2020a) The Future of Jobs Report – October 2020. [online] Available at: http://www3.weforum.org/docs/WEF_Future_of_Jobs_2020.pdf (accessed 28 October 2021).

World Economic Forum (WEF) (2020b) Our Education System is Losing Relevance: Here's How to Unleash Its Potential. [online] Available at: https://www.weforum.org/agenda/2020/04/our-education-system-is-losing-relevance-heres-how-to-update-it/?utm_source=sfmc&utm_medium=email&utm_campaign=2716680_Agenda_weekly-17April2020&utm_term=&emailType=Newsletter (accessed 28 October 2021).

Part 1

Which conditions nurture creativity?

1 What can we learn from people well-known for being creative?

It might seem obvious to say (a truism in fact) that fundamental to developing creative skills is having opportunities to find and hone them. Clearly though, this statement is not sufficient on its own (otherwise this would be a very short book). To understand what opportunities are necessary to nurture creativity we need to delve deeper. This chapter explores through the words of people well-known for their creative skills what opportunities they consider important to encourage creativity. Their insights, shared in conversations I have enjoyed with them, or that they have written in books or given in radio or television interviews, mainly take the form of childhood and early adult memories.

Exploring the insights of a number of creative people about what they think enabled their own creativity to flourish helps us to think about how to make similar experiences available for all children in and out of school. It is possible, by examining the common experiences of the creative people in this chapter that pertain to the development of their nascent creativity, to identify three conditions which come to the fore.

1. First, they all grew up in environments where the arts were valued as part of everyday life.

2. Second, they all talk about how they enjoyed having time to experiment with their ideas when they were young, some referring to this as playing.

3. And third, they all had positive experiences collaborating with other people.

The following subheadings look at these three 'conditions for nurturing creativity' (as I am calling them) in detail from the viewpoints of the creative people. By using their own words, I hope to convey some of the enthusiasm they expressed when sharing their creative journeys. You will see that the conditions frequently overlap. This only goes to highlight the holistic process creativity demands.

Valuing the arts in everyday life

Children's author Julia Donaldson is famous for her rhyming verse in books such as *The Gruffalo* and *The Smartest Giant in Town*. She explains, in a BBC documentary in 2020 celebrating her life and work, that her childhood home was a place '*where there was lots of music going on*'. She grew up in a house in North London with members of her extended family. Her mother was a keen member of a local choir and would always be singing in the house. Also, she says, '*my father played the cello, and the quartet would come to our house, so my sister and I used to give them their tea and their biscuits*'.

From an early age Julia wrote songs, including a musical version of *Little Red Riding Hood*. She remembers getting her family to act out the different parts.

> *My sister was Little Red Riding Hood. My mother was Wonderful Wolf. My father ruined it all as the Woodcutter by just sort of getting the giggles, and I was very very cross with him. I can still remember the songs.*

Julia wrote stories when she was young too. At home she remembers her granny cutting open big brown envelopes for her and her sister to draw and write on. At school, she recalls the first story she wrote was about a rabbit with ears that looked like carrots. She still finds acting out characters from her stories an important part of her writing process, and regularly gets her husband, grown up children and grandchildren to join in and help her.

For Julia Donaldson, living in a family home full of music and being exposed to the arts from a young age, at home and in school, were important to her creative development, together with the fact that her stories were taken seriously (apart from her father giggling as the Woodcutter!). This enabling environment for her creativity would lead to her being one of the most celebrated children's authors of all time.

The author Malorie Blackman, popular with young adult readers with her series *Noughts & Crosses*, and other novels such as *Pig Heart Boy*, similarly grew up in a house where she knew that the arts were taken seriously. In a BBC radio interview in 2017 Malorie talks about her early love of books. She describes how her mother introduced her to their local library in South London when she was six years old. The following week Malorie asked her mother if they could go again and was told '*Off you go then*'. So, she made herself a packed lunch and happily went to the library, on her own this time. To begin with Malorie would spend half a day at the library from time to time, '*then it was a full day. And I would just sit there reading, reading, reading*'. Malorie would take books home with her too. '*I devoured myths and legends from around the world … and anything I could get my hands on*'.

For Malorie, devouring books at her local library was '*a window onto the world*' that she says made her '*want to aspire to other things*'. She remembers starting to write stories and poems for her own amusement when she was around seven years old; something that she has loved doing ever since.

Both Malorie Blackman and Julia Donaldson have been Children's Laureates in the UK, advocating that children should read and write for pleasure. Both famous authors had upbringings which made them want to express themselves in their storytelling, and because the arts and creativity were valued in their families, then writing their own stories felt like a good thing to do.

The artist and Royal Academician Patrick Brill, known by the pseudonym Bob and Roberta Smith and for his colourful paintings depicting slogans such as *Make Art Not War* (1997) and *Art Makes Children Powerful* (2013), told me about his family home when he was growing up. 'Art was always all around us', he said, 'because both my parents were working artists'. He recalls his mother's work as being 'really joyous and lyrical' and thinks he shares her joy of 'just making a mark and finding that it makes you laugh in the way it does or does not describe something'. That humour, in making art, he finds has been very important in his own creative practice. Equally he has distinct recollections of his father's art. He would set off up a mountain to paint a landscape and be there all day, capturing the shifting light, Patrick remembers. It seemed like 'very hard work' and his style changed over time.

From a young age conversations about art happened a lot in the house. He thinks this might have been the case because his parents were also teachers – his father was the director of the Chelsea School of Art. Recounting a memory to me, Patrick spoke about when his mother drew him a picture of a Christmas pudding, asking as she drew what ingredients might go in it and who she should draw sitting around the table to eat it. The memory was clearly moving as it was a moment when he and his mother enjoyed being creative together, connecting through the art of drawing, and also through each other's fun responses to an imagined event.

In his book *You Are an Artist* (2020) he describes a similar dialogic encounter between himself and his daughter when she was very young focusing on a drawing she had done.

> The drawing did not look much like a giraffe, but she was proffering the idea that the marks she had made related to her love of giraffes (Etta is now, twenty-two years later, a successful graphic designer). Etta's giraffe was in a house. The house was represented by a square. I can remember the conversation: 'What does the giraffe eat?' 'Has the giraffe got a mummy and daddy?' 'Does the giraffe wear a dress?' Etta made drawings of all these elements. She then announced that the giraffe has a car, and a circle appeared as she made a vroom vroom sound, imitating the petrolhead giraffe speeding off into the sunset.
>
> (Smith, 2020, p 10)

Patrick Brill's mother had set time aside when drawing the Christmas pudding with him to let their minds wander, and he had done the same with his daughter. These encounters, between parent and child, openly place value on creativity in an everyday scenario.

The atmosphere in the family home of the award-winning performance poet Toby Thompson when he was growing up was also one where the arts were enjoyed on an everyday basis. When I asked him about whether he thought any particular experiences had helped his creativity to blossom, he spoke about his mother 'endlessly' reading him stories, and told me that both of his parents were in music bands. 'They didn't have careers in the arts ...

but they would play in gigs in pubs, and there were rehearsals happening in our house'. This sounds similar to what Julia Donaldson and her sister experienced.

> *I remember art and language and music, especially, being just like the air that we breathed. All of my memories of early childhood are connected to the songs that were being listened to in the house.*

Toby now sees his own work as a *'linguistic reflection'* of his parents' aesthetic taste, which he is *'very pleased to have inherited'*.

Like in Patrick Brill's childhood home, Toby Thompson recalls joining in with conversations about the arts with his parents. He particularly enjoyed sitting around the dinner table chatting about philosophical ideas, music, art, theatre and films. He felt these were *'implicitly valued'*. This high regard for the arts extended to Toby's mother taking him along to their local theatre (the Theatre Royal Bath) when he was 13 years old, where an open-mic evening had been launched to attract a wider demographic into the youth theatre group. This was the start of a long and ongoing relationship for Toby with, what is now called, the Egg Theatre – a theatre specially dedicated to young people's interests and talents in the performing arts (in Chapter 6 you can read more about the educational practice that takes place at the Egg Theatre).

> *So, I went along and performed with my keyboard. It was quite funny, as there were mostly slightly older teenagers, and [they were] mainly part of the Grime scene. But, it went quite well!*

This event was followed by hip hop artists being booked to perform, which led to the YPT Urban (a Young People's Theatre) company being set up, which Toby feels really fortunate to have been part of. He told me that *'it felt like an initiation'* and, although he enjoyed school, this gave him something outside of school that he sensed was *'more authentic'*.

By contrast, mathematician Marcus du Sautoy (who we heard from in the Introduction chapter) thinks being involved in drama and music at school was key to his creative development. When I spoke to him about what he considers to have been essential for nurturing his creativity, he said,

> *I think one of the most important things was the amount of extracurricular creative opportunities there were in my comprehensive school. I did a lot of music. We had an orchestra. I did a lot of theatre.*

He talked about *'falling in love'* with mathematics at around the same time as he started playing a musical instrument. This was when he was about 12 years old and his school took part in the School Mathematics Project (SMP) – an approach to mathematics that examines big ideas. Marcus saw a strong connection between this style of thinking about mathematics and the experiences he was having when acting and learning to play music. In these, he said, *'somebody has done some of the creation, but you move it on to add your own creativity to bring it alive'*. The SMP approach *'tapped into something that I had began to understand, which is that mathematics is a very creative place. It's a place where you can make worlds'*.

One of Marcus's mathematics teachers suggested that he read *A Mathematician's Apology* (1940) by G.H. Hardy. '*It's a lovely book. It really does talk about creativity in a mathematical realm*'. The argument made in the book is for mathematics to be pursued for aesthetic considerations, where its value is seen as independent of possible utility. '*That gave me the green light for mathematics being something that tied in with what I was enjoying, which was being creative in a musical or theatre context*'.

'*When I got to university, I continued all of these activities parallel to my [mathematics] studies*'. This included going along and working with Pegasus Theatre in Oxford. Like the Egg Theatre in Bath that played such a pivotal role in Toby Thompson's early creative career, Pegasus Theatre also has young people's interests and talents at its core. There, Marcus came across the international touring theatre company Complicité, with whom he still works alongside today in his role as the Simonyi Professor for the Public Understanding of Science at the University of Oxford. Complicité's creative approach brings together specialists from diverse fields, and Marcus has been involved with bringing to the stage a show called *A Disappearing Number* that tells the true story of a collaboration between Srinivasa Ramanujan and G.H. Hardy (the mathematician Marcus was introduced to by his school teacher), and a production titled *The Encounter* that explores through theatre the subject of consciousness.

So far, in this chapter it has been clear from the childhood memories described – whether through families having open discussions, or partaking in artistic pursuits including parents finding the time to be creative with their children, or through the promotion of opportunities – that the high value placed on the arts and creativity in the creative people's lives had a significant impact on their own sense of personal creativity at a young age. Conversely, the film composer Julian Nott believes his personal creative development did not start until much later in his life. Best known for scoring the music for Aardman Animations' *Wallace and Gromit* films, as well music for popular television programmes such as *Peppa Pig, Ben and Holly's Little Kingdom*, and *Lark Rise to Candleford*, he told me that although the arts were highly valued in both his home and at his school, he believes that in terms of '*creating things from nothing … with my own identity*' this did not begin until beyond university, where he studied music alongside philosophy, politics and economics.

> When I was a child or teenager … all my school years were about learning the piano, learning the organ, cello, learning things about music … it was about other people's creativity. … I used to write little pieces, but it was a game.

It was not until Julian joined the National Film and Television School, in London, after a short stint working in a management consultancy firm in the City, that he felt his own creativity was being nurtured. At the film school, he said, he responded well to the model of learning that was employed there, which he describes as a '*micro market*' approach. This included each student (of which there were only around 15 enrolled per year) being given a sum of money '*which was not insubstantial*' to make a film.

> If someone who was directing a film came to you and asked would you write the music for my film … you had to give them some of your money so they could raise

the funds to make the film … It was such an exciting time in my life, and I think other students would say the same thing, where you had this amazing opportunity to make a short film … and you just did it!

This way of working brought about his collaboration with fellow student Nick Park, who asked Julian to compose the music for Wallace and Gromit's first adventure *A Grand Day Out*. It is a partnership that has endured, entertaining millions of people around the world.

Julian Nott saw the creative process at the National Film and Television School as being very different from his learning experiences at school and university, where he felt opportunities for him to be personally creative had been largely absent. However, he also believes that the film school's methods *'wouldn't have worked if I hadn't had beforehand that formal training, because I would have floundered'*. Reflecting on whether he might have been creative earlier had digital music apps (such as GarageBand and Logic Pro) been invented, he said:

Everything would have been massively different if GarageBand was around when I was a teenager because I would have had more possibilities. Maybe I would have started composing then. I tried to compose when I was a teenager … but it was too difficult.

It is interesting how Julian refers to the *'little pieces'* of music that he wrote when he was a child in quite a dismissive way, as *'a game'*, yet now talks in terms of the *'possibilities'* that digital technology provides in being able to compose music without having to learn an instrument formally. His attitude towards experimenting seems to have shifted.

Time for experimentation and play

Having time to explore ideas is something that many creative people cite as an important part of the creative process. The people we have heard from so far in this chapter have undoubtedly relished having time in their childhoods to do this, sometimes thinking about different realities. We have heard how Julia Donaldson acted out with members of her family the characters that she created, something she still loves to do. As a young girl Malorie Blackman loved writing her own stories, and still does. Patrick Brill helped to conjure up imaginary and amusing worlds with his mother, and continues to inject the same kind of wit into his artwork. And Toby Thompson and Marcus du Sautoy expressed themselves when they were growing up through the performing arts, which they still enjoy doing in a professional capacity. Living a creative life, it seems, can begin early.

In the stories already told in this chapter, it is noticeable that there is a tension between, on the one hand, creativity being something that is playful, unstructured and fun, and, on the other hand, being something that is serious and life affirming. Patrick Brill, for instance, when talking about his mother's art, describes it as being *'joyous and lyrical'*, contrasting with how he saw his father's artwork as seeming *'very hard work'*. Toby Thompson mentions how he felt very fortunate to be part of the YPT Urban theatre group, but also uses the word *'initiation'* to describe what appeared to him to be a rite of passage. And Julian Nott talks about being at the National Film and Television

School as such an exciting time in his life, but clearly the atmosphere was one of challenge and intense hard work.

An artist who delights in engaging with this simultaneous juxtaposition of the playful yet serious nature of creativity in his work is the Royal Academician Anish Kapoor. Famous for his huge abstract public sculptures, such as *Cloud Gate* (2004) (nicknamed 'The Bean') in Chicago in the US, and *C-Curve* (2007) on the South Downs in Brighton in the UK, these massive, moulded mirror sculptures epitomise how creativity can be both light-hearted and profound.

Anish Kapoor explains in a 2009 BBC documentary about his work that although his parents were both '*extremely cosmopolitan*' and that '*music and art played a big role*' in family life, he saw his own aesthetic explorings as something that he '*just did*' when growing up, never imagining '*for one second*' that he would become an artist.

> *I mean, it didn't even occur to me. My mother dabbled in fashion and did some painting, but she could never finish anything. So, I would always finish them for her, which I loved doing. I loved making things, and I did that all through my childhood.*

This attitude of naturally embarking on a creative activity resulted in Anish attending art school, where he says he would never call himself an artist because he felt it was '*too big a responsibility*'. He is now one of the world's most sought-after sculptors of public art and still considers his creative routine as a spontaneous and evolving process, although he recognises that this way of working might make some people feel uncomfortable when they are striving to be creative themselves.

> *I think one has to have the courage to sit in an empty studio and wait for something to happen, and work and play and experiment, and try some daft ideas out. For me anyway, one has to dare.*

He demonstrates the playful process in a video promoting *The Great Big Art Exhibition* – an initiative announced in 2021 during the third Covid pandemic national lockdown in the UK. He is shown pushing some freshly squeezed paint around a blank sheet of paper with the side of a pencil, advising that '*allowing oneself to play in the simplest simplest manner*' is a good place to start when making an artwork. '*Art isn't always about having something to say*', he explains, '*sometimes it's about doing something and seeing what happens*'.

Anish Kapoor also says about his work '*there seems to be space for the viewer*', which is an invitation for us all to find our own meaning in his pieces. To do this we need to be open to the same playful modes of thinking that he uses to create them. Passers-by of all ages can be seen doing this when they watch their own reflections, and that of their surroundings, distort in the large silver surfaces of *Cloud Gate* and *C-Curve*. The sculptures are fun, while at the same time uplifting. They are works of art that tap into the viewer's need to try and make sense of what they are looking at – which, of course, is the world and their place in it.

The journalist and television presenter Andrew Marr is an amateur artist who has written about his artistic impulses in *A Short Book about Drawing* (2013). In it, he amusingly recounts a childhood memory of getting '*into trouble at home for drawing on white-painted walls – low down, behind chairs, where I thought nobody would notice'*. He continues, *'when asked what I wanted for a present, I would apparently say, "plain paper and pencils"'* (p 20). He recalls, when at school, because he could not sit still and listen to someone talking, he would shuffle towards the back row of desks. When there, *'I drew on my jotters. I drew in the margins of schoolbooks. I drew on tiny scraps of paper. I drew on the wooden desk'* (p 20).

Andrew Marr's desire to draw and paint has never left him, *'I can't help myself ... I draw most days, even if it's a doodle on the edge of a newspaper'* (p 10). As an adult, he enjoys getting out into the open air *'with a grimy bag full of oil paints and a canvas, or piece of wood'* (p 10). He confesses, *'Then, I am at my happiest'* (p 12). He views drawing and painting as:

> *a test of spirit, self-belief and of determination ... in both cases, I have been doing something that feels somehow stripped-down and essential; and for no other reason than the doing of it.*
>
> (Marr, 2013, p 19)

He remembers being given an art book by his parents about Van Gogh when he was about eight or nine years old.

> *The complete excitement about the colours, textures and wildness of Van Gogh's pictures remains uncontaminated now, more than 40 years later ... On went a very bright light bulb ... It must have been similar to the first time a musically attuned child hears Bach.*
>
> (Marr, 2013, p 20)

Some of Andrew Marr's distant relatives were professional and amateur artists, and when he was growing up he admired the original works of art by various painters on the walls of his family home that his parents would collect. He also remembers going to the annual Royal Scottish Academy exhibition as *'something of a family ritual'* (p 26). Hence, like the other creative people in this chapter, when Andrew was a child, there was a strong sense that the arts and creativity were appreciated by those around him. Similar to Anish Kapoor though, he saw his own art making as just something he enjoyed and needed to do; vehemently resisting, even as a child, the label of *'artist'*.

> *'So, you're an artist, are you?' That is what older relatives and friends say to kids who are beginning to delight in making pictures with pencils, and it can be patronising. An artist, we know, is someone with a High Calling, even aspirations to Genius ... Call yourself an artist? It's a little like challenging anyone who studies first-grade piano to compare themselves to Daniel Barenboim.*
>
> (Marr, 2013, p 25)

This is a noteworthy warning for us all to bear in mind when we make comments to children, or to anyone, about their creative outpourings, whether these are experimental, or attempts offered up as something more final.

Royal Academician artist Cornelia Parker, best known for her large installation pieces such as *Cold Dark Matter (An Exploded View)* (1991) and *The Distance (A Kiss with String Attached)* (2003), remembers being almost put off the idea of becoming an artist when she was growing up for a different reason. Although she could draw very well from a young age, and even enrolled to do a painting degree when she left school, she only became really interested in art halfway through this course when she realised that it could be more than just about being technically proficient. In a presentation to Oxford University students in 2017, she explained that until she was introduced to the conceptual sculptures of the artist Marcel Duchamp '*I was trying to find out what art meant to me*'. For Cornelia Parker, Duchamp, renowned for turning everyday objects into artworks by placing them in artistic contexts (most famously in 1917 putting a urinal on a plinth giving it the title *Fountain*), represented an entirely new way of being an artist. His work gave her the impetus and stamp of approval that she needed as an undergraduate to start experimenting with trying to convey in her art '*frictions between objects*', highlighting that every object has a cultural value. First of all, though, she had to change degree courses, from painting to sculpture. And because she was late in joining the sculpture course she missed out on learning some basic making techniques. Nevertheless, being technically limited did not restrict her creative output. In fact, she found that by experimenting on her own – investigating the properties of materials – she was able to acquire the inventive approach to sculpture she is now celebrated for, such as using an old shed for *Cold Dark Matter (An Exploded View)* (1991), and the offcuts of the red material used to produce Remembrance Day poppies in her *War Room* installation piece at the Imperial War Museum in 2015.

Unlike Anish Kapoor, where he does not always feel the need to say something in his work, for Cornelia Parker communicating ideas was, and still is, central. However, what they, and the other creative people in this chapter, have in common is the need to have the time and the freedom to let their minds wander, so they can play and experiment with their thoughts and with making things come about. It is a key condition that has enabled their creative development.

Opportunities to collaborate with others

The third condition creative people believe has nurtured their creative development when young involves them collaborating with other people. These interactions take different forms. Julia Donaldson and Patrick Brill talk about creative encounters happening when they enjoyed time with members of their own family – playing out their ideas, making them concrete, and building on and refining these in acts of togetherness. Creative collaborations are also apparent in the descriptions given by Marcus du Sautoy where he talks about his school orchestra and drama interests, and also in the support he had from his mathematics teacher, who steered him towards reading *A Mathematician's Apology*, a book that had an enormous impact on him.

The '*micro market*' model of learning employed at the National Film and Television School, which Julian Nott describes, was full of opportunities for creative collaborations, both in the making of films and when, as Julian told me, '*everyone reviewed your film when it was finished*'.

> *With that system you're in charge, so you assess the ideas or criticisms that come to you … it was up to you whether you accept advice or not from the other students*

or the teachers. … I think it made you a very creative person because you had to generate the ideas and the structure … and other people would react to your creativity … it cascaded the creativity because other people's creativity entered the picture and that generated more ideas from you … it was exhilarating.

In a wider community setting, a creative collaboration may take the form of an online group (such as those that proved so popular during the pandemic, like the Sofa Singers). More traditionally though, they come about when people join groups, like the youth theatres that Marcus du Sautoy and Toby Thompson benefited so much from.

Toby spoke to me about when he was a member of YPT Urban rehearsing with a director, a dance choreographer and a sound designer, as well as acting alongside other young people. He recalled how a London rapper known as Lowkey was especially commissioned by the youth theatre leaders to write a rhyming contemporary adaptation of Shakespeare's *Macbeth*. Toby remembered Lowkey leading some of the sessions. '*Suddenly I found myself within a group of people going through a collaborative experience that was quite intense*', he said. The resulting script, called *Macs and Beth*, was toured by YPT Urban around schools in the South West of England. Up to this point Toby had been writing on his own at home songs on the piano and rap separately. But he found that the whole theatre group collaborative process '*unlocked*' for him the realisation that he could perform in rhythm without a piano, and from there he developed his own distinctive craft.

Following the *Macs and Beth* school tour, YPT Urban raised around 10,000 pounds to take the show to the Edinburgh Fringe festival. The members did all the promotion work and the show received really good reviews. Toby was 15 years old at the time. While at the festival he also got to see the Bristol poet rapper Dizraeli, who Toby was '*just completely blown away by*'. So, after seeing his set for a second time, Toby went to talk to Dizraeli afterwards. This led to Toby getting invited to perform a five-minute poem at Dizraeli's next show and to supporting him at later gigs. '*There was a lot of kindness with him going out of his way to get me opportunities … He got me my first gig at Glastonbury*'. Toby also performed with Dizraeli and the poet Kae Tempest at the Royal Shakespeare Company.

Edinburgh Fringe also played an important role in the career of comedian and actor John Cleese. In his book *Creativity: A Short and Cheerful Guide* (2020) he writes about how one creative collaboration can lead to another. In it, he reveals why and how he joined a group called the Footlights, when he was an undergraduate.

I was at Cambridge [University] and I had got to know a very nice group of people who had a small club room near my digs … They put on little shows on the club-room stage, performing sketches and monologues and musical items. I didn't join the Footlights because I thought I might want to go into show business. Not at all! I was going to be a lawyer! I joined the club because its members were the nicest bunch of people I met at Cambridge.

(Cleese, 2020, pp 11–12)

To become a member of the Footlights, John Cleese had to write something to perform on the stage. He found writing a sketch to join enjoyable and comments that it was '*the first imaginative thing I was ever conscious of doing'*. He says, because everyone else there was also performing their own work he felt it was a *'friendly atmosphere'* and a *'perfect environment'* (p 13) in which to realise that he could be creative.

In these supportive surroundings John Cleese started to get to know and work with other members of Footlights on a show that toured to the Edinburgh Fringe. It was so successful it transferred to London's West End and led to international television appearances. The Footlights group was also where John Cleese met some members of the legendary comic troupe Monty Python, which also paved the way for him co-writing the classic comedy television sitcom *Fawlty Towers*. Other creative people who have been members of the Footlights include Stephen Fry, Emma Thompson, Alexander Armstrong, Germaine Greer and David Mitchell, to name a few.

Another perspective on a collaborative encounter is expressed by Anish Kapoor where he considers the importance of a viewer's interaction with a work of art he creates. If you remember, he says about his art, *'there seems to be space for the viewer'*. In the same way, Andrew Marr, in his book *A Short Book about Drawing* (2013), writes about how he perceives the relationship between an artist (in his case, Monet) and the viewer.

> *Without the viewer's ability to re-imagine the drawn lines, to take them in and possess them, and feed on them, so as to picture real trees by the real river, once upon a time ... Monet's drawing would be meaningless.*
>
> (Marr, 2013, p 74)

This echoes the idea Patrick Brill describes in his book *You Are an Artist* (2020) when he writes about the conversation he had with his daughter while she was drawing her giraffe. He saw their discussion in terms of a *'feedback loop'*, not just between himself and his daughter, but also with the wider world. He writes about all art being *'part of a huge societal feedback loop'* (p 13).

Similarly, from the standpoint of a reader, Marcus du Sautoy interpreted the words of G.H. Hardy in *A Mathematician's Apology* through his own experiences, taking from them what they meant to him personally, which gave Marcus *'the green light for mathematics being something that tied in with what I was enjoying, which was being creative in a musical or theatre context'*. And from an author's viewpoint, Julia Donaldson says at the end of the 2020 BBC documentary celebrating her work that she takes great delight in feeling part of *'something being passed from generation to generation'* when she receives stories written by children inspired by her books. The children find their own meaning in her work and move this on into something new of their own.

In conclusion, from the recollections of the creative people featured so far in this book, we have heard that having the arts and creativity in their lives from an early age opened their minds to the possibility of being creative themselves. By exploring what these creative people have to say about their own creative development we have been able to identify three conditions that are important for nurturing creativity: growing up in an environment that values the arts in everyday life; having time and allowing oneself to experiment and play; and collaborating with other people, in the various ways we have discussed. In the following chapters, we will examine these three conditions further by ascertaining if and how they are to be found in a variety of relevant theories and practices that have creativity as a central theme. Before that, in the next chapter, we remain with our enquiry into examining the life and work of creative people.

REFLECTIVE POINTS

- Do you have similar experiences to the people featured in this chapter that you believe helped to nurture your creativity? If so, what are these? Perhaps there are particular memories that stand out.

- Are there any opportunities described in this chapter that especially appeal to you?

- Toby Thompson says he has 'inherited' his parents' aesthetic taste. Have you inherited an aesthetic taste from anyone? If so, from whom and how would you describe it?

- Think about creative people that you admire and try to find out if they share similar experiences to the creative people in this chapter. Look to see if the experiences fall into the three conditions for nurturing creativity put forward in this chapter, or whether creating a new category is needed.

Further reading

Cleese, J (2020) Creativity: A Short and Cheerful Guide. London: Penguin, Random House.

Marr, A (2013) A Short Book about Drawing. London: Quadrille Publishing Ltd.

Smith, B R (2020) You Are an Artist. London: Thames and Hudson Ltd.

References

BBC (2009) Imagine: A Year of Anish Kapoor. [online] Available at: https://www.bbc.co.uk/iplayer/episode/b00p00f2/imagine-winter-2009-1-the-year-of-anish-kapoor (accessed 1 September 2021).

BBC (2020) The Gruffalo and Me: The Remarkable Julia Donaldson. [online] Available at: https://www.bbc.co.uk/iplayer/episode/m000qrxj/the-gruffalo-and-me-the-remarkable-julia-donaldson (accessed 1 September 2021).

BBC Radio (2017) Word of Mouth: Malorie Blackman on Language. [online] Available at: https://www.bbc.co.uk/sounds/play/b0952qq5 (accessed 1 September 2021).

Cleese, J (2020) Creativity: A Short and Cheerful Guide. London: Penguin, Random House.

Complicité website. [online] Available at: http://www.complicite.org/productions-home.php (accessed 1 September 2021).

Hardy, G H (1940) A Mathematician's Apology. Cambridge: Cambridge University Press.

Marr, A (2013) A Short Book about Drawing. London: Quadrille Publishing Ltd.

Smith, B R (2020) You Are an Artist. London: Thames and Hudson Ltd.

The Great Big Art Exhibition Pack (2020) Anish Kapoor Video. [online] Available at: https://firstsite.uk/content/uploads/2021/03/Firstsite-The-Great-Big-Art-Exhibition-Accessible-Pack.pdf (accessed 10 August 2021).

2 Other people known for their creativity

The artist Henri Matisse is frequently quoted (on posters and t-shirts and such) as saying *'Creativity takes courage'*. It is a great quote. Yet, how much does it really tell us about the nature of creativity? It is only when we unpick the specifics of creative behaviour that a deep understanding can emerge. By examining what many creative people experience, and by drawing together what they have in common, patterns can be spotted that can help us, as educators, plan effectively when aiming to *'teach for creativity'* (Durham Commission, 2019, p 98).

In the previous chapter we explored what some creative people believe helped nurture their talents. Now, we are going to consider the lives of other creative people from the perspectives of two academics: Ken Robinson, formerly professor emeritus at Warwick University and chair of the UK National Advisory Committee on Creative and Cultural Education (as discussed in the Introduction chapter); and developmental psychologist Howard Gardner, professor at Harvard Graduate School of Education. This time we can make use of the three conditions for nurturing creativity that we have already identified to assist our particular research enquiry into seeing whether the same, or similar, or perhaps different conditions can be detected from those experienced by the creative people in Chapter 1. In other words, we will be using the following conditions as lenses to look for patterns of behaviour: (i) growing up in an environment that values the arts in everyday life; (ii) having time to experiment and play; and (iii) collaborating with other people.

Robinson's 'Element'

In his book *The Element: How Finding Your Passion Changes Everything* (2009), Ken Robinson gathers stories about creative people to illustrate his belief that we are all born with *'tremendous natural abilities, and that we lose touch with many of them as we spend more time in the world'* (p xi). The aim of his book, he writes, is to offer a *'vision of human ability and creativity and of the benefits to us all of connecting properly with our individual talents and passions'* (p xiii).

In his 2006 TED talk *Do Schools Kill Creativity?* (that has been viewed over 70 million times in over 160 countries), Robinson blames the way that education systems are set up as one of the main reasons why many people never find their true talents. He thinks that on a worldwide scale young people's talents are largely *'squandered'* because there is a hierarchy of curriculum subjects, and the pecking order always leaves arts subjects at the bottom. This hierarchy, he explains, is based on the idea that those subjects at the top are judged to be the most needed for the workplace, and children are steered away from subjects they like on the grounds – *'don't do music, you're not going to be a musician'* or *'don't do art, you won't be an artist'*. He advocates that this point of view is *'profoundly mistaken'* and that *'creativity is as important as literacy'*. When I rewatched this TED talk, it struck me how similar Robinson's messages are to those expressed by Andreas Schleicher, Director of Education and Skills at the Organisation for Economic Co-operation and Development (OECD), when he advised the UK government's Education Select Committee in 2019 that *'Art may become more important than Maths'*. This was 13 years after Robinson's passionate, and clearly popular, plea about the need for arts subjects to be appreciated as being equally as important as 'core' curriculum subjects (as the English National Curriculum (2014) refers to English, mathematics and science). We return to what Andreas Schleicher has to say about creativity in Chapter 4.

Robinson's premise in *The Element: How Finding Your Passion Changes Everything* is that schools are not set up to help people find their true talents and therefore individuals never realise what they are capable of. He illuminates this position in the book with stories of people who have found their *'element'*. This we are told is a place *'where the things you love to do and the things that you are good at come together'* (p 8). Some people who he interviewed for the book, he tells us, *'revealed ideas and experiences they hadn't discussed in this way before'* (p xii).

In the case of Matt Groening, creator of the cartoon *The Simpsons*, Robinson writes about the compulsion Matt had to draw almost constantly when he was at school. Doodling kept him amused during lessons he found boring. This resonates with Andrew Marr's recollections of his childhood, described in his book *A Short Book about Drawing* (2013) (see Chapter 1). We are told Matt Groening most of all looked forward to his art lessons. Here he was allowed to indulge his artistic impulses by creating as many paintings as he liked with the art supplies freely available to him. His first-grade teacher, he remembered, would save the paintings that he did for years, and this inspired him to name the character Elizabeth Hoover in *The Simpsons* after her. Matt felt as he got older that his technical drawing abilities were not as good as he wanted them to be. However, his constant urge to draw encouraged him to look at the work of people who told funny stories using a cartoon style. One of these was John Lennon, famous for being one of the Beatles, but also for his books, like *In His Own Write* (1964), where he includes nonsense poems, short stories and drawings that were influenced by the humorous drawings of Spike Milligan and James Thurber. Such work inspired Matt to start making comics with a group of friends at school. They became more ambitious creating short films after going along to film nights together at their local university. For Matt Groening, this led to him getting a comic strip placed in a newspaper, followed by an invitation by Fox Broadcasting Company to pitch for a short animation slot, when famously the idea for *The Simpsons* came to him immediately.

Robinson calls Matt Groening's creative journey an '*epiphany*' story because it involved '*some level of revelation, a way of dividing the world into before and after*'. Such stories, he explains, illustrate how someone discovers the '*sweet spot for themselves*' (p 8). However, if we view Matt Groening's story through the conditions for nurturing creativity lenses we notice from Robinson's account that Matt's father was a cartoonist and filmmaker, so presumably when Matt was growing up he would have been exposed to the work of cartoonists and film-makers. This was before the age of the internet and apps, which make self-directed discovery easier. It seems, therefore, that Matt's environment was one where he was not only aware of the arts, but it is also likely to have been one where the arts were valued in everyday life. Also, we note that the school chosen for Matt to attend was '*a nontraditional school without grades or required classes*' (p 5) in which we hear he was given a great deal of freedom to indulge his need to draw and paint. This afforded the young Matt with lots of opportunities to experiment and play; our second condition for nurturing creativity. Furthermore, Matt's collaborations with his group of friends with similar interests seem to have been facilitated, to some extent at least, with the opportunity to view films at their local university, but also presumably with equipment so their collective comic and film ideas could come to fruition. So, it seems Matt Groening benefitted from all three of the conditions for nurturing creativity highlighted in Chapter 1 by other creative people. To be clear, I am not questioning whether Matt Groening is highly driven or talented – obviously he is because *The Simpsons* is the longest-running American animated series to date. However, I do query whether he found the '*sweet spot*' (his '*element*') by himself. The conditions for nurturing his talents were clearly in place, both at home and in the educational setting he attended. Could the school have done more to help nurture his talents? Perhaps. Apparently, he was bored in most of his lessons. Nonetheless, in Matt Groening's case what was provided was enough. Although, for other students more opportunities for being creative may have been needed to bring out their latent talents.

Another creative journey in Robinson's book that better illustrates how a particular school environment should have been more nurturing for a pupil focuses on the musician Paul McCartney, also a member of the Beatles. Robinson was involved in the early development of the Liverpool Institute for Performing Arts (LIPA), which is one of the leading facilities in Europe for training arts professionals, opened in 1996. The centre is housed in the building Paul McCartney went to school, and he is lead patron of the institute. On its tenth anniversary Robinson was invited to make a speech to the graduating students. He writes that he included ideas about '*the need to find your passion and talents, the fact that education often doesn't help people to do that, and that it often has the opposite effect*' (p 10). Paul McCartney responded with thoughts on his own school experiences. Robinson recalls:

> He said that he'd always loved music, but that he never enjoyed music lessons at school. His teachers thought they could convey an appreciation for music by making kids listen to crackling records of classical compositions. He found this just

as boring as he found everything else at school. He told me he went through his entire education without anyone noticing that he had any musical talent at all. He even applied to join the choir of Liverpool Cathedral and was turned down.

(Robinson, 2009, p 11)

This testimony is pretty shocking compared with how enormously successful and globally influential Paul McCartney has become with his musical talents. In contrast, in the same building, the approach to learning about music and other performance art forms now at LIPA (as detailed on the website) is to promote the virtues of belonging to a 'creative community' in 'a place of cultural courage' being 'creative mavericks'. This is done by replicating industry practice in a way not dissimilar to the experiences described in Chapter 1 by Julian Nott about his time at the National Film and Television School. At LIPA students are encouraged to focus on the 'synergy ... between performers, producers, managers, designers and technicians ... where learning is based wholly around conceiving and delivering events or products'. They refer to this as 'project-based learning', and acknowledge that 'interpersonal skills, like persuasion and negotiation, and understanding how groups can work well, are crucial'. These are the same complex social and emotional skills that Bakhshi et al (2015) named in their report *Creativity Vs Robots*, needed for being successful in our increasingly automated world (as discussed in the Introduction chapter). Paul McCartney's patronage of LIPA it seems is to set right his first arts education experiences, casting out old ways in favour of a creative education rooted in: valuing the arts in everyday life; time for experimenting and play; and opportunities for collaborating with other people.

References in *The Element: How Finding Your Passion Changes Everything* to Beatles members continue (Robinson is clearly a fan!) with a description of a creative collaboration between George Harrison (who went to the same school as Paul McCartney) and four other extremely successful singer-songwriters – Bob Dylan, Roy Orbison, Tom Petty and Jeff Lynne. We are told in the book that George Harrison's record company needed an extra track from him for a forthcoming record release. So, after coming up with the bare bones of a song he asked his four friends, who were all spending time together in Bob Dylan's studio in Los Angeles, to join him in singing the chorus. In Robinson's opinion the relaxed communal setting 'generated "Handle with Care", one of the most memorable songs of Harrison's post-Beatle career' (p 68). The friends obviously enjoyed the collaboration as they set about, in the wake of excited feedback from the record company, writing an entire album. It happened in the same spontaneous just-hanging-out-with-my-mates way, and sold over five million copies, leading to a second album. The makeshift band called themselves The Travelling Wilburys. The whole venture was, as the band's official website says, 'a happy accident', and photographs taken at the time indicate how much fun was had during the creative process.

Chance characterises many of the stories told in *The Element: How Finding Your Passion Changes Everything*. This includes the chance meeting of the choreographer Gillian Lynne with a psychologist when she was eight years old who advised her mother, after consulting him about why Gillian was having difficulties at school, to enrol her in a dance school. Gillian later went on to perform all over the world as a soloist in the Royal Ballet, formed her own musical theatre company, and collaborated with Andrew Lloyd Webber on the productions *Cats* and *The Phantom of the Opera*. An element of chance is also described in the creative journey of the actor Meg Ryan, who happened to be in the right place at the right time when a producer of an American soap opera spotted her in a commercial that she was in just to pay her way through studying journalism at university.

Similar fortuitous meetings, and the impact they had on creative people finding their path, are also apparent in some of the recollections shared in Chapter 1 of this book. Toby Thompson's mother hearing about, and taking him along to, the open-mic evening at the Theatre Royal Bath when he was 13 triggered subsequent collaborative encounters for Toby with the rappers Lowkey and Dizraeli. Julian Nott's collaborations with Nick Park from Aardman Animations happened because they were both training at the same place at the same time. And, Marcus du Sautoy was very fortunate to come across a mathematics teacher that both sparked his imagination and pointed him towards the work of G.H. Hardy who he thought might extend his interests further; subsequently leading to Marcus working on a production with Complicité. Although, by definition, these chance happenings could not have been planned for, they were enabled to some degree by the creative people being in environments where the three conditions for nurturing creativity were taken seriously.

Gardner's 'Anatomy of Creativity'

Another academic who has examined the lives of creative people is the developmental psychologist Howard Gardner in his book *Creating Minds: An Anatomy of Creativity Seen through the Lives of Freud, Einstein, Picasso, Stravinsky, Eliot, Graham, and Gandhi* (1993, reprint edition 2011). In it, he documents his study of these seven 'creative thinkers' (p 4). He firstly explains that although he found detailing their lives fascinating in themselves, he saw his work fundamentally to be a social science endeavour, rather than a humanistic one. His approach, therefore, was to look for 'concepts and generalizations that might *illuminate the study of creativity more broadly*' (p xv) by making comparisons between the lives. The research, he says, '*takes the form of a search for patterns – for revealing similarities and for instructive differences*' (p 7).

Gardner organised his study around three core themes, two of which focus on the impact other people had on the creative thinkers' lives.

> *1. The relationship between the child and the master* - In a developmental study, it is natural to look for continuities, as well as disjunctions, between the world of the talented, but still unformed, child and the realm of the confident master. Equally important in a study of creativity is sensitivity to the innovator's ways of drawing on the worldview of the young child.
>
> *2. The relationship between an individual and the work in which he or she is engaged* - Every individual works in one or more domains or disciplines, in which he or she uses the current symbolic systems or contrives new ones...

3. The relationship between an individual and other persons in his or her world - *Though creative individuals are often thought of as working in isolation, the role of other individuals is crucial throughout their development....*

(Gardner, 2011, p 8)

Above we read Gardner's reasoning for structuring his research around the three themes. He goes on to address his rationale for selecting which people to study. He wanted to consider the lives of people who were well-known for their *'breakthrough'* (p 6) acts of creativity and to look at talented people that helped to define the times in which they lived. He acknowledges that any shortlist of individuals will have its notable absences, and offers alternative names, *'why T. S. Eliot rather than Marcel Proust or Virginia Woolf? Why Mahatma Gandhi rather than Mao Zedong or Martin Luther King Jr.? ... '* (p 5). However, his decision, he explains, is based on *'an advantage in selecting a group of individuals who were roughly contemporaneous'* (p 7). This meant that he could comment on the particular era that formed them, and which they helped to form. Gardner also justifies his choices with the hope they *'constitute a representative and fair sample'* drawn from different *'domains'* (p 6). By taking as subjects the neurologist and psychologist Sigmund Freud (1856–1939), the theoretical physicist Albert Einstein (1879–1955), the painter Pablo Picasso (1881–1973), the composer Igor Stravinsky (1882–1971), the poet T S Eliot (1888–1965), the dancer Martha Graham (1894–1991) and the political and spiritual leader Mahatma Gandhi (1869–1948), Gardner's hope was to study the people who provided the creative breakthroughs of the *'modern era'* (p 6).

In the findings section of the book, Gardner discusses *'which lessons'* from his analysis *'hold for the study of creativity in general'* (p 333). After clarifying that other academics may draw different conclusions about the same people, depending on how they interpret the case studies, or if they have additional knowledge about the individuals, he proposes the idea of *'a portrait of the Exemplary Creator'* (p 334). Gardner tells us this portrait emerged over the course of the study through him being struck by how much the creative thinkers had in common. He outlines the lengthy portrait using female pronouns, naming her EC. Statements about her early years include: *'EC's family ... value learning and achievement, about which they hold high expectations'* (p 334); *'EC's areas of strength emerged at a relatively young age, and her family encouraged these interests'*; and

> *There comes a time when the growing child, now an adolescent ... feels a quickening impulse to test herself against the other leading young people in the domain.*

(p 335)

These observations resonate with our three conditions for nurturing creativity, apparent in the lives of the creative people we looked at in Chapter 1 of this book. What is more, when we delve into the details of each case study in Gardner's book, these conditions become further supported.

Taking the first condition, it is evident from Gardner's descriptions that many of the homes of the creative thinkers were ones in which the arts were valued in everyday life. We hear that Pablo Picasso

> was strongly encouraged by his father, who was himself a practicing artist and teacher of the art form; and had surpassed his father and other local masters by the time of early adolescence.
>
> (p128)

T S Eliot's mother 'was a poet of considerable ambition and some talent who considered herself a failure because she had not completed her formal education' (p 213). Martha Graham's father

> liked to play music and to sing for Martha and her two sisters ... Her mother, Jane Beers, was a tenth-generation descendant of Miles Standish, the Puritan figure immortalized in Henry Wadsworth Longfellow's poem 'The Courtship of Miles Standish'.
>
> (p 250)

The second condition for nurturing creativity – of having time to experiment and play – is also apparent in the case studies. Indeed, Gardner argues that his research shows that creative breakthroughs come about through 'an intersection of the childlike and the mature; the peculiar genius of the modern in the twentieth century has been its incorporation of the sensibility of the very young child' (p 7). Perhaps this point is most obvious in the abstract paintings of Pablo Picasso where he reimagines the world in basic shapes and bold colours. Upon reading the case studies we also come to appreciate what might have enabled the childlike perspectives of the other creative thinkers to persist and develop into their adult work. For instance, we are told that Albert Einstein's curiosity was piqued by the electrical appliances his father manufactured for a living, 'he was fascinated by wheels and all other objects with moving parts' (p 86). In Einstein's autobiography he apparently recalls his father showing him a compass when he was four or five years old and being perplexed why the needle did not move even when the case was rotated. Gardner tells us that the young Einstein 'posed gritty questions and then pondered them at length'. Gardner suggests that 'such questions are reminiscent of the type that young children have always posed – at least those youngsters who are not habitually "shut up" by elders' (p 84). This comment demonstrates how Gardner identifies an atmosphere where one is allowed the freedom to question and think aloud as congenial to nurturing creativity and associates this condition with Einstein's upbringing. And certainly, it was Einstein's questioning of contemporary scientific thinking that led to his breakthrough theories, because when setting himself problems to solve he started with first principles.

The third condition for nurturing creativity – having opportunities to collaborate with other people – can likewise be found in the extensive descriptions of the creative thinkers in various respects. One example is in the way that the adolescent Einstein was influenced by a medical student that 'his family offered regular hospitality to'.

> *Talmey took a liking to the young Einstein and gave him many books to read, including such classics as the works of Kant and Darwin. Noting the youthful Einstein's interest in physics, Talmey also furnished popular books on force and matter. Particularly influential was a series of volumes by an Isaac Asimov-like polymath named Aaron Bernstein. Apparently, Einstein absorbed from these books not only much factual information but also a basic scientific worldview.*
>
> (Gardner, 2011, p 87)

The mutually respectful ongoing relationship that Einstein had with Max Talmey when he was lodging with the family meant that Einstein's evolving interests could be built on and expanded. This could be described as an experiential learning experience. We will discuss this concept in the next chapter when we look at educational theory.

Conversely, Gardner sheds light on how the activities of Sigmund Freud as a prolific letter writer to friends and family when he was a young man puts him in the role of the influencer. '*Already he is the teacher – reporting what he has learned, asking pointed questions of his correspondents, and seeking to synthesize knowledge*' (p 51). Freud was fond of the theatre, he went to art exhibitions and was well-read in the classics, as well as philosophy. So, in his letters '*equipped with a developing imagination*' he was able '*to invent scenes, characters, institutions, and flights of poetic fancy*'. Here we see all three of our conditions for nurturing creativity in action. Gardner adds, '*One infers that his correspondents got the better end of the epistolary bargain*' (p 51).

Similarly, Gardenr tells us about how T S Eliot entertained and informed readers when he was a young man through his writing. '*He issued his own newspaper at school, stocking it with jokes*' (p 215). Here we are reminded of Matt Groening making comics and animations with his school friends. Andrew Marr (whose book about drawing we discussed in Chapter 1) also mentions how he produced cartoons for '*university newspapers and left-wing magazines*' (2013, p 28). I wonder how T S Eliot, Matt Groening and Andrew Marr would have utilised digitial technologies if they were available when they were at school. They might have entertained and informed audiences via a school radio station or YouTube channel.

Both Freud and Eliot are considered by Gardner to exemplify what he terms as a dominance in '*linguistic and logical intelligences*' (p 336). Here he applies his theory of Multiple Intelligences (or MI theory), which is a framework he developed that attempts to describe an array of largely discrete human intellectual capacities, and which Gardner offers as a critique to the view that there is a single type of intelligence – one that can be measured by IQ or other short answer tests. Although there is certainly great merit in the way that this theory challenges a standard view of intelligence, it has unfortunately sometimes been used in educational environments to label pupils, which should be strongly avoided as this can have a negative impact on development. Nevertheless, Gardner's conclusion in *Creating Minds*, where he finds that the creative thinkers '*differ from one another not only in terms of their dominant intelligence but in terms of breadth and the combination of intelligences*' (p 336), sheds a positive light on how a variety of strengths are equally relevant when it comes to being creative.

Gardner's work draws attention to the fact that we always need to firmly bear in mind that creativity is vitally important across skills sets and subject domains and is not simply the preserve of the arts. Indeed, many creative breakthroughs that have had the widest impact on our lives have been made by scientists, mathematicians and engineers, such as Edward Jenner, William Farr, Florence Nightingale, Ada Lovelace, Alan Turning, Tim Berners-Lee and Isambard Kingdom Brunel, to name only a few. Improvements in life expectancy (doubling in less than a century) have happened due to creative thinking in areas such as developing vaccines, data analysis and better healthcare practices. In recent years, innovations in engineering and communication technology have meant change on a scale previously unseen. However, it is not without some irony that the creative efforts of those in the computing world have led to the increasing automation that currently necessitates a rapid response in the education sector to prioritise teaching for creativity.

REFLECTIVE POINTS

- Ken Robinson's book *The Element: How Finding Your Passion Changes Everything* (2009) focuses on his view that schools are not set up to help pupils find their talents. Is this your experience?

- Do you think you have found your '*element*' (as defined by Ken Robinson)? If so, what is it?

- Howard Gardner studied the people who he considered provided the creative breakthroughs of the '*modern era*'. Do you agree with his choices? Who would you select if you were to undertake a similar study?

- Think about people working in areas other than the arts and find out if they have anything to say about:

  (a)   enjoying the arts;

  (b)   experimenting and playing with ideas; and

  (c)   collaborating with other people.

- Then, think about whether they might use these experiences to inform their work in a creative way.

Further reading

Gardner, H (1993, reprint 2011) *Creating Minds: An Anatomy of Creativity Seen through the Lives of Freud, Einstein, Picasso, Stravinsky, Eliot, Graham, and Gandhi*. New York: Basic Books.

Robinson, K (2009) *The Element: How Finding Your Passion Changes Everything*. London: Penguin Books.

References

Bakhshi, H, Frey, C and Osborne, M (2015) Creativity Vs. Robots: The Creative Economy and the Future of Employment. [online] Available at: https://media.nesta.org.uk/documents/creativity_vs._robots_wv.pdf (accessed 28 October 2021).

Department for Education (DfE) (2014) *The National Curriculum in England: Framework for Key Stages 1–4.* London: HMSO. [online] Available at: https://www.gov.uk/government/publications/national-curriculum-in-england -framework-for-key-stages-1-to-4 (accessed 16 August 2021).

Durham Commission (2019) Durham Commission on Creativity and Education. [online] Available at: https://www.dur .ac.uk/resources/creativitycommission/DurhamReport.pdf (accessed 28 October 2021).

Gardner, H (1993, reprint 2011) *Creating Minds: An Anatomy of Creativity Seen through the Lives of Freud, Einstein, Picasso, Stravinsky, Eliot, Graham, and Gandhi.* New York: Basic Books.

Lennon, J (1964) *In His Own Write.* London: Vintage Books.

Liverpool Institute for Performing Arts (LIPA) website. [online] Available at: https://lipa.ac.uk/ (accessed 2 September 2021).

Marr, A (2013) *A Short Book about Drawing.* London: Quadrille Publishing Ltd.

Robinson, K (2006) Do Schools Kill Creativity? *TED Talk.* [online] Available at https://www.ted.com/talks/sir_ken _robinson_do_schools_kill_creativity?language=en (accessed 3 February 2021).

Robinson, K (2009) *The Element: How Finding Your Passion Changes Everything.* London: Penguin Books.

The Travelling Wilbury's official website. [online] Available at: https://www.travelingwilburys.com/ (accessed 2 September 2021).

Conclusion to Part 1

As we have seen, many of the creative people featured in Chapters 1 and 2 have experienced similar conditions when growing up and although they come from a range of different backgrounds, with different interests, it has been possible to connect their experiences through the three conditions for nurturing creativity. Sometimes the conditions were made available to the creative people in their home environment, other times in their schooling or in a community setting. Some people had very privileged upbringings, others would have had their creative journeys severely disrupted if it were not for good access to local libraries, arts services and education.

In the next part of the book we examine what consensus there is among theorists who concentrate on themes relevant to nurturing creativity, and how their theories tie in with the conditions we have been using as lenses so far.

Part 2

What consensus is there on how to nurture creativity?

3 Finding consensus on conditions for nurturing creativity across theoretical frameworks

In this chapter we will be looking at the theories of various academics whose work touches on the subject of creativity to some significant degree. It is not intended to be a definitive survey, but an attempt to underpin with previously developed educational theory the conditions for nurturing creativity that I have so far argued in favour of.

In this section of the book, from the outset, I should declare my allegiance to John Dewey's theories. His clarity of thought and lucid descriptions of an 'experiential continuum' (1938) and 'art as experience' (1934) never fail to resonate with my own experiences as an educationalist. So, this is where we will start.

Dewey's experiential continuum framework and theory on aesthetics

Philosopher and psychologist John Dewey was working in America at the beginning of the twentieth century. With his experiential continuum theory (1938) he set out to develop a framework to address issues that he observed in the teaching methods in American schools at a time of mass industrialisation. He saw two distinctive school systems, terming them 'traditional' and 'progressive', claiming both as 'miseducative' (p 37). His belief was that the approaches to teaching and learning that he found in traditional schools imposed subject matter and rules in a way not conducive to positive learning experiences. Conversely, he thought that the principles developed in progressive schools were in direct opposition to traditional schools, and therefore, according to Dewey, they emphasised the freedom of the learner at the expense of learners benefiting from the wider experiences of adults. His experiential continuum framework sought to explain and deal with these issues. In it he describes how 'every experience both takes up something from those which have gone before and modifies in some way the quality of those which come after' (p 35). He illustrates the importance of prior experience for further learning by describing how traditional and progressive school systems do not allow for such opportunities because the former does not seek pupils' prior experiences and the latter does not help pupils to expand on prior experiences with the insight of an adult's wider experiences.

Dewey proposes that because one experience influences the next it is crucial in an educational environment that experiences are 'worthwhile' (p 33). He explains that learning methods should be encouraging and flexible, rather than imposing and rigid. In order to demonstrate this point, Dewey describes a miseducative traditional school environment as one where the teaching principles are 'autocratic and harsh' (p 34), where 'the subject matter of education consists of bodies of information and of skills that have been worked out in the past' (p 17) and that are 'imposed' on those 'growing slowly towards maturity' (p 19). He says the atmosphere is one where there are 'standards and rules of conduct' where 'moral training consists of forming habits of action in conformity with these rules and standards' (p 18). He explains how the traditional schools are 'sharply marked off from other social institutions' (p 18) saying they have patterns of organisation that include 'time-schedules, schemes of classification, examination ... [and] ... rules of order' (p 18). This environment, Dewey believes, raises two critical problems: (i) the widening of pupils' experience is problematic when the gap between pupils' own prior experience and what is being imposed is too great; and (ii) the learning described in such a regime does not allow for pupils to contribute towards their learning. He contrasts this organisation with ordinary family life. Dewey puts forward the argument that the attitudes of pupils in a traditional school 'must, upon the whole, be one of docility, receptivity, and obedience' and that

> books, especially textbooks, are the chief representatives of the lore and wisdom from the past, while teachers are the organs through which pupils are brought into effective connection with the material.
>
> (p 18)

He says, 'teachers are agents through which knowledge and skills are communicated and rules of conduct enforced' (p 18). In this learning environment, Dewey asks, 'How shall the young become acquainted with the past in such a way that the acquaintance is a potent agent in the appreciation of the living present?' (p 23).

Dewey proposes that learning needs to fall 'within the scope of ordinary life-experience' (p 73) so that there is 'active participation by the pupils in the development of what is taught' (p 19), where there is a 'widening' of 'external conditions' for 'subsequent learning' to take place (p 38). This is what he means by a continuum (or continuation) of experiences. He believes that this accumulation of experiences will lead to 'growth' (p 36), which he views as mental, moral and physical. Dewey goes on to contrast positive experiences with ones that retard growth in different directions, commenting that the effect of the latter is to 'shut off the person' (p 36).

Embedded throughout Dewey's experiential continuum theory is the notion that learning needs to be considered as complex and holistic when teaching methods are designed. He tells us that because the 'criterion of education as growing' lies in experiences that 'open up avenues for development' (p 38), there needs to be an understanding that by connecting experiences over time, habits, expectations and mindsets are developed. This includes '*the formation of attitudes*' and this '*covers our basic sensitivity and ways of meeting and responding to all the conditions we meet in living*' (p 35).

Additionally, Dewey claims that in a learning environment that does not value the continuation of experiences, opportunities are missed for experiences to be '*a moving force*' (p 38) for learning. He explains that by connecting experiences pupils' curiosity is aroused and their initiative strengthened. In his theory on aesthetics (*Art as Experience*, 1934), which he never specifically links to his theory on experiential learning, he says this drive forward comes from our desire to find '*stability*' (p 18). Dewey tells us that the stability we crave is our impulse to find out about the world, and that this process '*is not stagnation but is rhythmic and developing*' (p 18). He describes how '*equilibrium comes about not mechanically and inertly but out of, and because of, tension*' (p 13), suggesting that our human need to make sense of our surroundings manifests in how we spontaneously react every day with the world when our senses are stimulated, and that these experiences are aesthetic in nature. He illustrates this point with an example of a man who pokes a fire to make it burn better being '*fascinated by the colorful drama of change enacted before his eyes and imaginatively takes part in it*', and how therefore '*he does not remain a cold spectator*' (p 3).

The main consideration for Dewey in the designing of teaching methods is involving the learner in the process of planning in order to encourage a strong sense of personal commitment and engagement. He describes this as involving the learner in the '*formation of the purposes which direct his activities*' (1938, p 67). Figure 3.1 illustrates how this works, as explained by Dewey in his experiential continuum framework. This process is holistic because it involves the learner's capacity for curiosity, rooted in their own life experiences, being aroused by an initial '*impulse*' (p 67) (the source of curiosity) that is '*a moving force*' (p 38) for learning. Therefore, the process concerns how an individual acts on their thoughts and feelings.

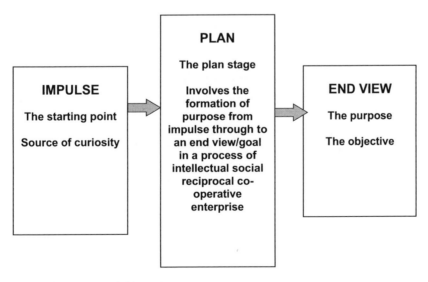

Figure 3.1 *Dewey's experiential learning process.*

Dewey explains that 'a genuine purpose starts with an impulse' (p 67) and an impulse results in an action or an idea. He defines 'purpose' as an 'end-view' (p 67) (which can also be described as the end goal or objective). In a simple example he uses the situation of a baby seeing the brightness of a flame and having the impulse to touch it (touching it being the purpose). In another example he describes the impulse of a man to build a house after seeing a prime piece of land. Dewey explains that the 'plan' stage (p 71), which bridges the impulse to the end view, 'involves foresight of the consequences which will result from acting upon the impulse' (p 68). It is the stage, he tells us, of 'intellectual anticipation ... it gives direction to what is otherwise blind' (p 69). It is the stage where the accumulation of experience would prevent, in the example of the baby, it from being burnt. In the case of the man and his house, the transmission of impulse to a finished building requires the formation of many judgements based on his experience. Dewey says that this stage needs the person to stop, look, listen, but also to understand the significance of what they see and hear. The significance is the understanding of the consequences that will result when what is seen and heard is acted upon. In unfamiliar cases, we reflect on past experiences and form a judgement of what to expect. Therefore, the formation of purpose is a 'complex intellectual operation' (p 69).

In a classroom situation, this process takes place in a reciprocal social context between pupil/s and teacher. Dewey describes very clearly how this works in practice.

> The way is, first, for the teacher to be intelligently aware of the capacities, needs and past experiences of those under instruction, and secondly, to allow the suggestion made to develop into a plan and project by means of the further suggestions contributed and organized into a whole by the members of the group. The plan, in other words, is a co-operative enterprise, not a dictation. The teacher's suggestion is not a mold for a cast-iron result but is a starting point to be developed into a plan through contributions from the experience of all engaged in the learning process.
> (Dewey, 1938, p 72)

For Dewey, a vital point is that pupils learn best through a process of 'social intelligence', which he describes above as a 'co-operative enterprise' (p 72), and this enterprise includes the experiences of everyone involved, the pupils and their teacher/s, and hence produces more commitment and engagement from all. This addresses Dewey's criticism about teachers in traditional schools only being 'the organs through which pupils are brought into effective connection with the material [subject matter worked out in the past]' (p 18). In his critique on progressive schools, which he believes were developed in direct opposition to traditional schools, he sees as an important educational problem the lack of concentration on the process of 'social intelligence' (p 72) in the plan stage, and therefore teachers seeing impulses as purposes, and acting on impulse alone.

Dewey carries forward his argument on the learner's involvement in the 'formation of the purposes which direct his activities' (p 67) into asking how much, and how little, direction a pupil needs from a teacher in both the conception and the execution of an activity. He frames this question as an ethical one. He asserts that the relationship between teacher and pupil is such that, first, there is a moral right for a child not to have the wider insight of an adult withheld. Second, the relationship needs to be one where an *'adult can exercise the wisdom his own wider experience gives him without imposing a merely external control'* (p 38). Dewey demonstrates the difference between excessive external control and a lack of direction for the learner with comparisons in his observations of how traditional schools impose learning and how

> *newer schools tend to make little or nothing of organized subject-matter ... to proceed as if any form of direction and guidance by adults were an invasion of individual freedom.*
>
> (p 22)

By emphasising the balance between the learner's need for direction with their need to have some degree of control of their learning, Dewey seeks teaching approaches that promote epistemological growth. That is to say, teaching that assists the learner in understanding how they learn by understanding how knowledge is constructed (ie constructivist approaches).

Having now examined Dewey's experiential continuum theory in some detail, let us turn to considering how his ideas correspond with the conditions for nurturing creativity that we identified in Part 1 of the book. First, how do his ideas relate to valuing the arts in everyday life?

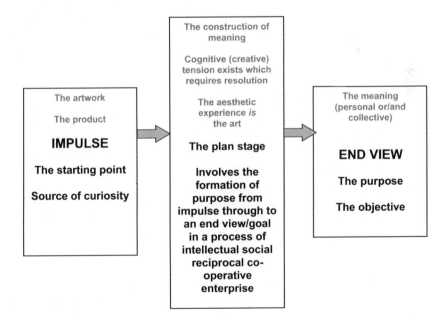

Figure 3.2 *Dewey's experiential learning process mapped onto Dewey's aesthetic experience process.*

By coupling Dewey's theory on experiential learning and his theory on aesthetics (see Figure 3.2), which both share the common notion that humans need to make sense of the world, our understanding about valuing the arts in everyday life, and how this improves our personal creative development, is deepened. In essence, Dewey argues that art should not be perceived as something that exists separately from us. He explains that our engagement with a work of art – which he names as 'the product' (1934, p 222) – is the same as our engagement with anything else in the world that arouses our curiosity. For Dewey, the arousal of curiosity is itself an aesthetic experience because when we engage with the world through our senses (as previously explained) our attempt to satisfy our curiosity plays out in a cognitive process that 'is not stagnation but is rhythmic and developing' (p 18): 'Equilibrium comes about not mechanically and inertly but out of, and because of, tension' (p 13). Passarelli and Kolb (2012), drawing on the work of Dewey, describe this as 'creative tension' in their four modes model of experiential learning because it moves 'back and forth between opposing modes of reflection and action and feeling and thinking' (p 72).

According to Dewey, therefore, the experience of looking at a work of art, or indeed hearing one, *is* art; hence the title of his book *Art as Experience* (1934). It is while grappling with cognitive (creative) tension, which craves resolution (equilibrium), that meaning is constructed by the viewer (or listener). This paradigm explains why we intuitively ask ourselves when engaging with art, 'what does this work of art mean to me?' It is the same point Anish Kapoor makes (see Chapter 1) when he says 'there seems to be space for the viewer' in his artworks. Also, the notion appears in Andrew Marr's *A Short Book about Drawing* (2013) where he describes how he sees the relationship between an artist and a viewer. And Patrick Brill writes about the same idea in *You Are an Artist* (2020) when he explains art as being 'part of a huge societal feedback loop' (p 13).

When engaging with and deliberating about art in a group setting, the overall question is similarly 'what does this mean to us?' This is exemplified in Marcus du Sautoy's comment when talking about being part of his school orchestra and drama group: 'somebody has done some of the creation, but you move it on to add your own creativity to bring it alive' (see Chapter 1). The original music score or play script is the artwork/source of curiosity/impulse/starting point, but the group brings it alive through their joint efforts (in the plan(ning) stage) where each individual brings something to the piece that blends together into something new (the end view). We might say that the end view is co-constructed, and indeed this term is often used for collaborative creative encounters.

Central then to Dewey's theories is his respect for individual thought and expression, and for individuals to be given opportunities to exercise these. Therefore, his experiential framework explicitly promotes our second and third conditions for nurturing creativity, that of having time for experimentation and play, and providing opportunities to collaborate with others. To recap, such a sense of personal agency is evident where he insists on the inclusion of pupils in the formation of their own learning. Although, when he questions how much, or how little, direction pupils need from their teachers, he makes it clear that the 'wisdom' of those with '*wider experience*' (1938, p 38) is needed. His model of learning rests on the principle of '*reciprocal co-operative enterprise*' in a setting '*where the teacher is intelligently aware of the capacities, needs and past experiences of those under instruction*' and where the teacher's suggestions are not '*cast-iron*', but instead are starting points '*to be developed into a plan through contributions from the experience of all engaged in the learning process*' (p 72). The experiential process is experimental.

Again, if we recall some of the educational experiences of the creative people in Part 1, we can envisage them belonging to the same, if not similar, model of learning. For instance, the '*micro market*' approach that Julian Nott talked about at the National Film and Television School very closely follows the same model. In this case, the source of curiosity/impulse/starting point was self-selected/generated by the students, who then chose (and persuaded) who they wanted to work with in the plan(ning) stage. This involved working through ideas together towards the end view (which was a film), the content of which was not predetermined by the tutors. Toby Thompson rehearsed with a director, a dance choreographer, and a sound designer, as well as with other young people, at the Theatre Royal Bath. The source of curiosity/impulse/starting point (and artwork) for these sessions was the *Macs and Beth* script written by the rapper Lowkey. The rehearsals were the plan stage, involving the formation of purpose from impulse (the script) through to the end view (a finished play to tour to regional schools) in a process of '*reciprocal co-operative enterprise*' (p 72) because what the play was going to look like was unknown until it was ready to be performed. The play was taken to the Edinburgh Fringe, also not originally foreseen at the start of the process but formulated as an idea by the group during the process. These two examples recognisably relate to Dewey's experiential continuum framework, as does, in a less formal way, Patrick Brill's description in Chapter 1 about his mother drawing for him a Christmas pudding. From the initial impulse of the pudding theme they both shaped the end image, which was only part of the end view. The other (main) objective was presumably having an enjoyable time together chatting about their fantasy festive feast. Perceiving this experience in a structured way may feel contrived, but it is nonetheless useful as it highlights the potential of a seemingly modest experience on a child's creative development, and points towards possible comparable interventions.

In contrast, Dewey's experiential framework reveals how not following the three stages leads to a learning experience that is impoverished in terms of nurturing creativity. Where Dewey talks about there being a lack of concentration on the process of '*social intelligence*' (p 72) in the plan stage, this is as a consequence of teachers treating the source of curiosity/impulse/starting point as the end view. The resulting constraints on learners' input (of something of themselves) into the formation of their work limits opportunities for personal individualism to be developed and demonstrated in outcomes. This is a theoretical explanation for Ken Robinson's (2009) premise that young people's talents are largely squandered in schools. It also explains why Paul McCartney did not enjoy his music lessons, and why, as Howard Gardner (2011) points out, habitually telling youngsters to 'shut up' is not conducive to creativity (as discussed in Chapter 2).

My own research (Hosack Janes, 2021) into the design of curriculum activities exposes the same concern. A study I undertook in the UK with 25 teachers across five primary schools uncovered the extent teachers planned for pupils to input their own thoughts and ideas into their work. I analysed the learning activities teachers planned and the diversity of the pupil outcomes in relation to each activity. I found that the learning activities which were more teacher-led and instructional were very end-view-driven (or we might say product-driven, although Dewey's use of the word 'product' is different and means artwork). Hence, these activities did not follow the experiential continuum framework stages, as described by Dewey. Pupil outcomes from these product-driven activities were either almost identical to their teacher's demonstrations (or in some cases the demonstrations of an art practitioner), or very similar to the teacher's work and/or other pupils' work. This meant that outcomes showed very little evidence of pupils' individual voices; so therefore it can be concluded that pupils' creative development was curtailed, rather than enhanced, by the activities planned by their teachers. Conversely, it was found that if a learning activity was planned that embraced opportunities for teacher–pupil co-operative exchange in a process that bridged, rather than omitted, the source of curiosity/impulse/starting point stage and the end view, pupil outcomes were more diverse, exhibiting genuine originality for each pupil. This process-led teaching and learning approach was understood therefore to develop an individual's creativity more effectively than the product-driven approach. The study was based on an arts education scheme called Take One Picture, run by the National Gallery, London, and is discussed further in Chapter 5.

Vygotsky's sociocultural theories

Like Dewey, the work of psychologist Lev Vygotsky is highly relevant to the subject of nurturing creativity. He writes specifically about imagination and creativity in childhood and draws our attention in his sociocultural theories to how meaning is socially co-constructed. He formulated his theoretical frameworks in Communist Russia from the 1920s until 1934. Due to his untimely death from tuberculosis some of his theoretical ideas are incomplete, leading academics to anticipate his thoughts. Unlike Dewey, whose writings are in English, Vygotsky's work is written in Russian, so most people (myself included) rely on translations, complete with inevitable interpretation problems that can occur when no direct comparisons for words exist.

Vygotsky's theories cover language development, how cultural systems both shape and are shaped by humans, and the search for methods to study psychological change. He proposes that the sets of beliefs which underpin how humans communicate and act are shaped by social, cultural and historical factors, and consequently these are worth analysing as they form personal identity.

Vygotsky scholar Harry Daniels (2016) warns us that

> the concepts developed by Vygotsky sometimes appear as a web of tightly related notions. Breaking into this web of understanding is not easy. The

network of cross-referencing requires a prior understanding before entry into the network!

(p 32)

Bearing this in mind, we shall look first at Vygotsky's ideas in relation to how he thinks people make sense of the world.

In essence, Vygotsky tried to explain how we deal with living in a world which is humanised. That is, he describes how we live in a world of objects and actions where the meaning of these is culturally constructed in social settings, which are historical in origin. Therefore, Vygotsky sees meaning as coming about through social interactions, where meaning takes up something that has previously been ascribed to the objects and actions. Connections can be made here with how Dewey describes the accumulation of experiences for the individual: *'Every experience both takes up something from those which have gone before and modifies in some way the quality of those which come after'* (1938, p 35).

Introductions to the humanised world, in Vygotsky's view, are through sociocultural mediation; a process that involves how something is presented to someone, where language, numbers, signs, symbols and art are all conceived as psychological devices that have influence on the individual. If we, as Daniels does in *Vygotsky and Pedagogy* (2016), take the example of teaching a child to read, Vygotsky would think about this as a series of experiences. First, the experience a child has of the world mediated by adults. Second, an adult's experience of the world mediated through a text. Third, the goal for a child to read independently, therefore becoming someone whose experience of the world is mediated by the text. We can see in this example that control – over choice of book, selection of subject matter and use of language when talking about the book – is with the adult reading with the child. Through the social activity of reading together the objective is to transfer control of the activity to the child. However, because the world is also being mediated through the text (the choice of subject matter, use of language, and imagery too if there is any), a degree of control resides with the author of the book, and indeed the culture they belong to and have been brought up in.

This oft-quoted description (below) by Vygotsky from *Mind in Society: The Development of Higher Psychological Processes* further explains how a social activity, like the reading scenario (above), fits into a theoretical framework:

> *Every function in the child's cultural development appears twice: First, on the social level, and later, on the individual level; first between people (interpsychological), and then inside the child (intrapsychological). This applies equally to voluntary attention, to logical memory, and to the formal concepts. All the higher functions originate as actual relations between human individuals.*
>
> (Vygotsky trans., 1978, p 57)

This multilayered, complex sociocultural, historical theoretical understanding of how meaning is constructed can be applied to all human interaction. Activity theory (eg

Engeström, 1999) is a post-Vygotskian development that uses such an understanding to investigate human behaviour. From a Vygotskian perspective, Daniels (2016) tells us 'the social/cultural/linguistic mediation of meaning serves to create a range of individual possibilities for understanding' (p 10). This awareness can help us appreciate how the complex nature of mediation enables individuals to arrive at different understandings; understandings that shape individual viewpoints and personalities.

The question of control (or agency), and with whom it resides, is particularly important when it comes to thinking about nurturing an individual's creative development. Social constructivists, like Dewey and Vygotsky, are often talked about in relation to other constructivists who also focus on the internal mental processes of individual knowledge construction, such as Jean Piaget and Jerome Bruner. For these latter constructivists 'social environment and social interaction work merely as stimulus for individual cognitive conflict'. Social constructivists like Dewey and Vygotsky, on the other hand, shift their focus to view the social environment as central to knowledge construction. For social constructivists, therefore, learning is perceived as largely being 'situation-specific and context-bound' (Hua Liu and Mathews, 2005, p 388). With this line of thinking it could be claimed that an individual has little control over knowledge construction. However, we can see from Vygotsky's quote on the previous page that the relationship between the social context and the individual is one where they are not separated, rather an individual's agency is part of an integrated relationship.

For Vygotsky, 'the critical issue', Daniels says,

> is with respect to whether the resources that a collective culture embodies are regarded as fixed offerings from which the individual selects or they constitute the starting points for negotiation.
>
> (2016, p 42)

Here are echoes of Dewey's experiential learning model where

> the teacher's suggestion is not a mold for a cast-iron result but is a starting point to be developed into a plan through contributions from the experience of all engaged in the learning process.
>
> (1938, p 72)

Such an environment, as we have already discussed, is conducive to our second and third conditions for nurturing creativity.

Daniels puts forward an example of a culture where the 'offerings' for individuals are more 'fixed' (2016, p 42) where he discusses children's work on display boards in schools (p 160–170). He argues that such practice is 'part of the system of signs that constitute the culture ... and through these acts of publicity the principles which regulate the curriculum are revealed' (p 160). Daniels shows a scenario where a high amount of control over pupils is clearly what is expected with much of the pupils' artwork looking very similar from one to the next. Alternatively, he points out, when pupils' work on display boards is more varied, the level of control within the school culture is exhibited to be much lower. There are strong parallels here with my own research (Hosack Janes, 2021), described previously, where I explore the nature of teaching and learning in both teacher-led activities and ones that employ experiential features; the findings make a connection between pupil outcomes that are more diverse and greater cognitive challenge and creative agency for pupils.

Vygotsky assists our understanding of creative development with his explanation of how *'the plasticity of our neural substances'* (trans., 2004, p 8) *'gives rise to'* two distinctive types of activity: *'Reproductive'* activity (p 7) and *'combinatorial or creative'* activity, which includes *'imagination'* (p 9). Detailing the first, he tells us:

> *Any human act that gives rise to something new is referred to as a creative act, regardless of whether what is created is a physical object or some mental or emotional construct that lives within the person who created it and is known only to him. If we consider a person's behaviour. ... One type of activity we would call reproductive, and is very closely linked to memory: essentially it consists of a person's reproducing or repeating previously developed and mastered behavioural patterns or resurrecting traces of earlier impressions.*
>
> (Vygotsky trans., 2004, p 7)

Vygotsky goes on to call his memories of the house he lived in when growing up *'traces of the impressions'* he formed in childhood, likening these memories to drawing or writing activities where *'I am merely reproducing what exits in front of me or what I have mastered and developed earlier'* (p 7). He believes *'such retention of previous experience'* is *'significant'* *'in a person's life insofar as it facilitates his adaptation to the world around him'* (p 8). However, he continues:

> *the brain is not only the organ that stores and retrieves our previous experience, it is also the organ that combines and creatively reworks elements of this past experience and uses them to generate new propositions and new behaviour. If human activity were limited to reproduction of the old, then the human being would be a creature oriented only to the past and would only be able to adapt to the future to the extent that it reproduced the past.*
>
> (Vygotsky trans., 2004, p 9)

Therefore, in Vygotskian terms, creative thinking is synonymous with growth in the same way Dewey sees *'growth'* (1938, p 36) as coming about through the personal accumulation and *'widening'* (p 38) of experiences.

If we turn now to Vygotsky's concept of the *'zone of proximal development'* (ZPD) (trans., 1978) – arguably his most well-known theory – we see his ideas around mediation are used to explain how a child's motivation benefits and development is accelerated *'under adult guidance or in collaboration with more capable peers'* (p 86). This theory was Vygotsky's search for a method of assessing psychological development, particularly focusing on how a learner can form higher psychological functions from lower ones. He views the intellectual process of collaboration in his ZPD theory as one in which those under instruction see the relevance of, and can make connections between, what they currently understand and the next steps of development, to be explored with guidance. In this sense ZPD echoes Dewey's insistence that learning needs to fall 'within the scope of ordinary life-experience' (1938, p 73), and for it to be widened for subsequent learning to take place.

In his last major work, *Thinking and Speech* (trans., 1987), Vygotsky sums up his thoughts on ZPD and how the nature of learning changes depending on the type of guidance/control given to the learner:

> *Instruction is only useful when it moves ahead of development. When it does, it impels or awakens a whole series of functions that are in a stage of maturation lying in the zone of proximal development … this is what distinguishes instruction of the child from the training of animals. This is also what distinguishes instruction of the child which is directed towards his full development from instruction in specialized, technical skills such as typing or riding a bike.*
>
> (Vygotsky trans., 1987, p 212)

Daniels's (2016) example of pupils' work on school display boards where they are facsimiles of each other would undoubtedly align with the '*technical skills*' type of instruction in Vygotsky's quote above. And, in relation to my own research findings (Hosack Janes, 2021), Vygotsky's '*technical skills*' most accurately conveys the nature of teacher-led (product-driven) pedagogy, rather than the experiential (process-driven) activities.

Daniels (2016) points out that for Vygotsky the more knowledgeable '*supportive other*' (p 59) in a ZPD pedagogical relationship does not have to be physically present. This raises questions about the meaning of the word 'social'. For example, can the author of a book that inspires a learner to explore more about a subject he or she is interested in be viewed as a '*supportive other*' (for example, G.H. Hardy for Marcus du Sautoy, or Aaron Bernstein for Albert Einstein)? Does it matter if the author is no longer alive? Can discussion with the reader take place simultaneously on the page and in the mind of the reader through the posing of open questions (as I am aiming at here)? Even though the reader is interacting with the text, does this constitute a dialogue, whereby one viewpoint or suggestion feeds off and into another (as in Dewey's '*co-operative enterprise*' (1938, p 72) description)? For this to happen does content need to be mediated by the physical presence of the other/another person? Is this a more accurate understanding of social interaction? And how does social interaction and the co-construction of meaning/knowledge work online?

Craft on possibility thinking and little 'c' creativity

Anna Craft (2013) considers the internet and the relationship young people have with digital cultural spaces as being an arena for '*possibility thinking*' (PT). Craft (2000, 2001, 2002) describes possibility thinking as involving a shift in a learner's thinking from asking 'what is this and what does it do?', when encountering something they are unfamiliar with, to 'what can I do with this?' She proposes PT is central to creative learning, concluding that digital cultural spaces are *'potent'* spaces with potential for *'problem finding, question posing, imagination and combinational play'* (p 126), arguing that *'creative digital engagement'* has four key 'P' features:

Possibility thinking *(transforming what is to what might be – with particular reach in a digital context),*

Plurality of identities *(in relation to activities, people, places, literacies)*

Exploratory **P**layfulness and dialogic

Democratic **P**articipation

(Craft, 2013, p 128)

We can see from these features that the first and third relate directly to our experimenting and play condition for nurturing creativity. The fourth 'P' relates to our condition for promoting opportunities for collaborating. And the second 'P' could enable the valuing of the arts in everyday life.

Craft suggests all the above digital environment features offer children and young people opportunities to produce, as well as to consume, culture. And it is certainly true that examples abound on the internet of individuals posting written content, uploading visual images, sharing musical compositions, and alike. In this book we have heard how Julian Nott believes *'everything would have been massively different'* for him as a composer if apps such as GarageBand and Logic Pro had been around when he was a teenager. He commented, *'I would have had more possibilities'* (see Chapter 1). As well as making music possibilities, this would have included sharing possibilities.

In my book *Using the Visual Arts for Cross-Curricular Teaching and Learning* (Hosack Janes, 2014) I write about a *'cycle of creativity'* (p 100) when I describe how museum, gallery and archive websites connect *'people across time, place and cultures'* when they encourage users to upload their own responses to collections.

An original inspiration *(such as a highly accomplished masterpiece or ancient artefact) can inspire a personal response. When this is shared with others online, it has the potential of being viewed by many thousands of people from across the world. This response can then become the inspiration itself for others to respond to. And so the cycle continues.*

(Hosack Janes, 2014, p 100)

Content production and consumption on the internet is not only centred on the arts, of course, but also to social action campaigning and thought exchanges about all manner of things. Craft tell us that for young people

such opportunities arguably have special potency because they engage with the developmental needs of young people for self-expression, exploration of personal identity, extension of peer relationships and striving towards independence.

(Craft, 2013, p 128)

According to Craft, PT is enhanced by the enormous range of content on the internet: Horizons are expanded and numerous voices on diverse subjects can be found. Yrjo Engestrom (2012), a post-Vygotskian activity theorist, explains that multiple voices in a culture is a sign of strength and richness, because when problems need solutions there are different perspectives to call on. However, how content is presented for PT to be encouraged is important.

Daniels's (2016) analysis of Vygotsky's theories help our understanding here where he talks about whether the 'resources' of 'a collective culture' are 'regarded as fixed offerings from which the individual selects' or constitute 'the starting points for negotiation' (p 42). If digital content is understood to be a stimulus 'starting point to be developed into a plan through contributions from the experience of all engaged', as Dewey describes 'co-operative enterprise' (1938, p 72), then agency over the co-construction of meaning/knowledge/ culture could be argued to be democratic (ie control over content in a dynamic digital space is governed by the user/s). But if some content is presented as fixed truths, where the word of the assumed knowledgeable other is unquestioned, then the digital world in this instance resembles more the teacher-led 'dictation' Dewey (1938, p 72) warned about. Alan Rusbridger, former editor of *The Guardian* newspaper, in his book *News and How to Use It* (2020) notes his concern about readers being able to distinguish between opinion (a point of view for possible consideration) and 'justified belief' (p 79) (something more fixed).

Where Craft talks about digital spaces being 'potent' places for young people 'striving towards independence' (p 128), we are also reminded of the Vygotskian scenario of reading with a child. The goal is for the child to read independently. To achieve this a text is mediated by an adult who selects and reads it to the child. Moreover, the chosen text is an interpretation of the world according to the author, who is shaped by the culture they belong to. Digital spaces similarly offer content that is pre-selected and interpreted for the user. However, due to the remote quality of the internet (sometimes with recorded content, other times with live content to mass audiences) the nature of mediation on the whole is different. Unless the digital space is utilised for one-to-one or small group interaction, the experience is less personal than an adult sitting next to a child sharing a book.

Craft's collaborative research focusing on pedagogy and PT in the classroom reveals that

> teachers and learners enter a co-participative process around activities and explorations, posing questions, identifying problems and issues together and debating and discussing their thinking.
>
> (Cremin et al, 2006, p 4)

Pedagogical practice shown to foster PT is reported in the research as teachers 'standing back' and positioning themselves so that they can notice learners' engagement and intervene in a timely fashion with probing 'what if?' questions, 'enabling learners to gain agency' (p 7). We are told 'it was considered [by the participating teachers] important that the children were involved in jointly determining the direction of their work' (p 8). And 'creating time and space' was a feature of PT pedagogy where 'learners ideas were taken seriously, independence encouraged ... and time flexibly handled' (p 9). In one example the '*speculative stance*' of a teacher was used to indicate '*genuine interest in the children's ideas*' and the teacher's language was commented on as helping the children '*maintain a sense of agency and influence over their work*'. Craft and Chappell (2014) propose that the '*inclusive environment*' PT pedagogy enables is one where:

(i) '*Children's experiences and ideas are highly valued*';

(ii) '*Dialogue between children and between children and teachers is encouraged*';

(iii) '*An ethos of respect is nurtured and children as well as teachers experience meaningful control, ownership, relevance, and innovation in learning*'.

(Craft and Chappell, 2014, p 409)

These PT experiences are conducive to all our conditions for nurturing creativity. Yet, a legitimate question remains as to whether, and to what extent, such a personal educative process can be accommodated in a digital space without the intervention of a physical presence.

Coupled with Craft's concept of PT is her development of '*little c creativity*' (or LCC) (Craft, 2001). She proposes that because '*individuals are required to be increasingly self-directed*', due to the '*intensification of change*' (p 45) in society (citing changes in social structures, the economy and in technology), it is helpful to view everyday creative behaviour differently to the creativity displayed by those that are more creatively accomplished, which she and others call '*high creativity*', also known as '*big c creativity*' (p 46).

She sees the realm of big c creativity as having '*certain characteristics, such as innovation/ novelty, excellence, recognition in the field within which it takes place and a break with past understandings or perspectives*' (p 46). Here, she acknowledges big c creativity as values related, ie belonging to a sociocultural landscape, seen by Vygotsky as a key part of the mediation process (as previously described) involving the construction of meaning/ knowledge.

Craft's research into little c creativity with young children is influenced by the approach taken by Howard Gardner in his study of the lives of Freud et al (1993, reprint edition 2011) (see Chapter 2). Craft picks up on some of the common factors Gardner identifies in these creative thinkers; namely, how they are '*productive each day*' (p 372) and the '*incorporation of the sensibility of the very young child*' (p. 7) in their work: A characteristic that ties into our second condition for nurturing creativity – having time to experiment and play.

Craft argues that little c creativity behaviour (which is not confined to children but applies equally to everyone's everyday creative behaviour) includes the generation of alternative ideas that '*enables individuals to find routes and paths to "travel" in many aspects of their lives*' (2001, p 46). The main attribute for little c creativity is being open to ideas so that new personal goals can be set. This involves '*problem identification as well as problem-solving*' and affects a person's ability to '*move on*' (p 51), echoing how Dewey (1938) and Vygotsky (trans., 2004) articulate growth. Craft (2001) adds, '*a person with high LCC enters life situations with an attitude of "What if?" – which implies a positive open approach to possibilities that could develop'* (p 55). We can see here how the concept of little c creativity dovetails with the concept of PT.

Craft's model for little c creativity is a developmental one. She proposes that *'the more successful experience of LCC an individual has, the more likely they are to operate in this way in other contexts'* (p 52). She suggests that a person's cultural context affects how readily they are able to exercise little c behaviour, depending on whether it is valued or not. She gives the example of a national context *'where choice and personal autonomy are severely reduced'*. The same restrictive environment in a school or home could also limit the ability of someone to generate and experiment with their own ideas. Similarly, in an organisation where there is much prescription and control over day-to-day routines, a worker would be less able to act on their own decision-making. This is akin to how Dewey talks about experiences that *'shut off the person'* (1938, p 36), and where Gardner comments on issues associated with habitually telling the young to *'shut up'* (2011, p 84).

Specifically, Craft (2001) puts forward a number of overlapping 'qualities' which are necessary for little c creativity to take place.

(i) 'Self-determination and direction ... to enable personal route-finding' (p 56).

(ii) 'Development' that moves things on to a 'new place' (p 57).

(iii) 'Action' and 'Depth' because 'unless one recognizes what it is that one has done either in ideas or action, the result cannot be said to be truly creative as opposed to serendipitous' (p 57). The suggestion is that the awareness comes about through concentration.

(iv) 'Risk', as in 'not knowing how one's ideas may land or turn out'. Craft gives as examples 'trying out a new combination of food for a meal' and 'a musician trying a new career path' (p 57).

(v) 'Posing questions' because they are 'at root about openness and possibilities' (p 58).

(vi) 'Play', because when 'being open ... playing with ideas and new possibilities/ combinations' is 'logically necessary' (p 58).

(vii) 'Innovation', where this involves 'doing something differently' (p 58). Craft sees this as a spectrum where at one end it could be something that is 'novel to the child, but not necessarily to the wider world', and at the other end 'ideas and actions which are novel in the eyes of the wider field' (p 56).

(viii) 'Being imaginative', because 'an outcome that is not novel or unexpected could not be considered to be a product of LCC' (p 58).

The emphasis on originality in the last two qualities concurs with Vygotsky's notion that *'new propositions and new behaviour'* result from *'combinatorial or creative activity'* (trans, 2004, p 9) (as previously described). Craft's emphasis also supports the findings of my own research (Hosack Janes, 2021) that reveals pupil outcomes exhibit more originality when pedagogy is experiential (process-driven) (as also previously described).

Craft's little c/big c model is useful when thinking about conditions needed for nurturing creativity, with many of the qualities that she proposes as little c behaviour echoing the three broader conditions for nurturing creativity that we are discussing in this book; albeit mainly stressing the second condition of having time for experimentation and play.

Using Craft's own criteria for big c creativity – having *'certain characteristics, such as innovation/novelty, excellence, recognition in the field within which it takes place and a break with past understandings or perspectives'* (p 46) – she would undoubtedly assign to this category the achievements of the creative people featured in Chapters 1 and 2. Nevertheless, she would view many of their experiences that set the path for their big c accomplishments as little c behaviour that set the path for their big c accomplishments.

Kaufman and Beghetto (2009) point out having a little c category is *'useful for addressing common misconceptions about creativity … for instance, too much focus on big c leads to the idea that only certain people can be creative'* (p 3). However, they feel there is room for *'more nuanced levels of creativity'* (p 2), offering their own *'four c model of creativity'* (p 1).

First, they propose the addition of a *'mini c'* category *'designed to encompass the creativity inherent in the learning process'* (p 3). They define mini c as *'the novel and personally meaningful interpretation of experiences, actions and events'*, linking this new addition to Vygotsky's sociocultural processes of interpreting the world within mediated contexts (as discussed in this chapter). Even though the descriptions outlined by Craft accommodate this, they suggest that if the little c category is the only option to *'classify students'* creative insights' then *'a fourth-grade student learning about the planets'* with *'unique and personally meaningful insights'* will have to be *'lumped in with those of an astronomy graduate, or even a professional astronomer'*, and therefore *'the fourth-grade student is held, even implicitly, to unfair standards'* (p 4). This reminds me of what Andrew Marr recalls feeling when older relatives and friends said to him *'So, you're an artist, are you?'* (see Chapter 1), when he/they associated the term 'artist' with more grandiose callings. However, for me, Craft's little c/big c divide seems to serve well enough.

The same argument, to resolve apparent issues with the wide little c spectrum, is used by Kaufman and Beghetto to add a *'pro-c'* (p 4) category, which is set aside for the aforementioned professional astronomer and other professional experts. However, for me this again seems to overcomplicate, taking attention away from the qualities needed to enable creativity (useful for increasing opportunities) at the expense of endeavouring to assess and classify the type of creativity being demonstrated.

As we have so far seen in this chapter, constructivist theories rely on the learner building knowledge through their interaction with their surroundings, guided and mediated by others in some way, which may, or may not, leave a lasting positive impression on the individual. The multifaceted complexities in these relationships have brought about protracted and continuing debate over which pedagogical methods are most effective. Heated disputes focus on both the purpose of education and on how much direct instruction pupils should be given by their teachers. At the core of such debates is where one believes the balance should be struck between helping pupils pass tests and exams that are heavily 'fact' or 'knowledge' based, and providing opportunities that enable pupils to learn the skills they need to think and learn for themselves – in other words, utilising our natural human capacity to be curious, to think creatively around subjects and problems, and to come up with novel ideas. This debate is sometimes set up as a dichotomy between the direct teaching of facts/knowledge (as in the traditional schooling methods that Dewey described) and no teaching at all ie letting pupils find their own way. However, each of the theorists we have looked at so far fundamentally avoid promoting a dualistic approach, instead describing a notion of guided learning, where the relationship between the learner and teacher is one of respect for each other's abilities and prior experiences and where there is an understanding that knowledge is a sociocultural construct.

Let us now look at some other theorists who think along the similar lines. Each of them, in the same way that I have a particular attachment to Dewey's work, have been championed by one or more of the creative people featured in Part 1 of this book. For example, Margaret Boden is championed by Marcus du Sautoy in his bestseller *The Creativity Code: How AI Is Learning to Write, Paint and Think* (2019); Mihaly Csikszentmihalyi's flow theory is discussed in Andrew Marr's *A Short Book about Drawing* (2013); and Guy Claxton's ideas on creativity are favoured by John Cleese in his book *Creativity: A Short and Cheerful Guide* (2020).

Boden's three types of creative thinking

Cognitive scientist Margaret Boden argues that knowledge and creativity are not opposed to each other, and actually '*creative thinking cannot happen unless the thinker already possesses knowledge of a rich and/or well-structured kind*' (Boden, 2001, p 95). Like Craft's little c/big c division, Boden makes a distinction between everyday creativity and creativity that is highly accomplished. In respect to creativity that entails coming up with ideas that are new in the whole of human history, Boden assigns the label '*H-creativity*' (where H stands for historical). She names coming up with ideas that are new for the individual '*P-creativity*' (where P stands for psychological) (Boden, 2010, p 30). For Boden, the separation of creativity into these two categories is essential for trying to understand the process of creativity in the individual mind. She points out that understanding the process is important for teachers and psychologists because they

> *need to know how children and adults can think up valuable ideas that they had not thought before (and perhaps even could not have thought of before), and how they can be helped to do so.*

She adds, '*If some of those ideas are also new in the historical sense, and even valuable enough to be recorded in the history books, all well and good*' (2001, p 95).

She goes on to explain how '*the cognitive psychology of creativity asks where those new ideas come from, and what mental processes are responsible for producing them*', proposing that there are three types of creative thinking: '*combinational*', '*exploratory*' and '*transformational*'. All of these differ in how they are '*grounded in previous knowledge*' (p 96). Combinational creativity, as the name suggests, involves combining (or associating) ideas, new and old, in unfamiliar ways. Boden says this is the case in poetic imagery, analogy, and in the visual arts by literally overlaying images with collage techniques. Exploratory creativity happens when someone has been taught the relevant rules of a particular activity or concept and then is enabled to investigate '*possibilities inherent in the space*'. This could be, for example, learning the rhyming rules in a verse, or the rules of colour theory, the rules of physics or the periodic table. Boden writes,

> *Countless people earn their living by means of exploratory creativity: run-of-the-mill lounge-pianists and graphic artists, mundane jazz-musicians, and many workaday scientists.*
>
> (p 96)

Transformational creativity exists when some of these rules are broken. Boden points out that '*even Mozart had to familiarize himself with the contemporary musical style for ten years before he came up with anything interestingly new*' (p 102). Here she highlights that H-creativity is historical because it is influenced by the creativity of others, and is therefore part of a tradition, even if this is subverted. And historical because the idea is worthy of being '*recorded in the history* books' (as Boden comments above).

Boden tells us that both exploratory and transformational creativity '*arise out of some culturally accepted style of thinking, or structured conceptual space, that the person has learnt – and, to some extent, mastered*' (p 96). Thus, she acknowledges the significance of sociocultural influences and a balance between direct instruction and time allowed for experimentation and play. Where Boden gives advice on how not to '*smother*' creativity, she talks in terms of avoiding (i) '*an unbending insistence on the "right" answer*' or '*right*' way of doing something; (ii) '*an unwillingness (or inability) to analyse the "wrong" answer to see whether it has some merit*' and (iii) '*an expression of impatience, or (worse still) contempt, for the person who came up with the unexpected answer*' (p 98). Avoiding these, Boden believes, will increase the self-confidence of the learner in their own ability to have good ideas, which will lead to them trying out more ideas.

Boden also gives advice on how to help learners decipher whether, or not, their own ideas are good through an evaluation of accepted styles and concepts. The awareness of the value of a creative idea was also a key consideration for Craft (as we have seen in her qualities of little c creativity), and was included as a key aspect in the National Advisory Committee on Creative and Cultural Education (NACCCE) definition of creativity, previously discussed in the Introduction chapter. Boden recommends that learners compare the ways in which two things are similar and different. She suggests that whether one or the other is better may be hotly contested, but whether and why one is '*at least sensible*' in relation to the other is '*interesting*' and '*fruitful*' (p 101). One example she gives where this might work well is in a cookery class where children are encouraged to follow the rules of a recipe, but to try out alternative ingredients that might work, or not – swapping raspberry jam for another flavour jam, or perhaps mustard! An added benefit to expressing one's likes and dislikes like this is to practise making stylistic judgements explicit, underpinning them with justifications.

Overall, Boden gives us a clear rationale for why learning rules is important, but also how the way in which these are presented – not as *a fait accompli* – is vital for creativity to be supported. The memories of Julian Nott and Marcus du Sautoy in Chapter 1 resonate here. For Julian he did not feel empowered to create his own music until well into his 20s despite studying at a very high level the creativity of much celebrated composers. Perhaps if the pedagogy he experienced at school and university had allowed for the three types of creative thinking Boden puts forward he might have had the confidence to start composing earlier. Marcus du Sautoy, even though he did not compose his own music, he says he felt part of the creative process when playing other people's work in his school orchestra. It seems to me this was because he, and the other members of the orchestra, were encouraged to make the music their own – to follow the rules but to play about with how they performed the pieces together – the same being true of his drama experiences at school.

Boden sums up her theory using the following aphorism:

> Freedom of creative thought is not the absence of constraints, but their imaginative – yet disciplined – development. 'All work and no play' does indeed make Jack a dull boy (and Jill a dull girl, too). But 'all play and no work' is just as sterile.
>
> (Boden, 2001, p 201)

Csikszentmihalyi's theory of flow

The people in Part 1 of this book articulate their creative journeys with a real sense of joy and passion. Their creative work is clearly something they find fully absorbing and love doing. Indeed, Marcus du Sautoy talks about *'falling in love'* with mathematics. For these creative people the enjoyment their activities of choice bring them is less about relaxing and switching off, and more about intensifying their thinking and doing things that are personally life affirming. The activity channels their energy into something that they consider to be extremely important. The psychologist Mihaly Csikszentmihalyi calls this type of immersive experience *'flow'*: A metaphor for *'effortless action'* many people feel *'in moments that stand out as the best in their lives'* (Csikszentmihalyi, 1997, p 46).

Finding one's flow activity (or, if you are lucky, activities), or helping others to find theirs, is a wholly worthwhile ambition. According to Csikszentmihalyi, finding your own flow space (or zone – being 'in the zone' as people say) can *'improve the quality of life'* and *'making sure that the conditions of flow are a constant part of everyday life'* is important (p 47). This is irrespective of whether someone can, or wants to, make a living out of their flow of activity/activities.

There are distinct parallels between Csikszentmihalyi's flow space, Boden's (2010) concept of P-creativity, and Craft's (2001) concept of little c creativity. All focus on acknowledging the significance of human behaviour that is rewarding, challenging and that can happen regularly in the right conditions. Exploring what those right conditions are, and making sure they are available to those who are being nurtured, is the subject we are exploring in this book. There are also very obvious links, if you remember from Chapter 2, with Ken Robinson's notion of the element, which he writes about finding, describing it as a place *'where the things you love to do and the things that you are good at come together'* (2009, p 8). His argument is that people's gifts and passions are largely squandered because schools are not set up to help people find their true talents.

Csikszentmihalyi's flow theory is based on extensive empirical research over decades starting in the early 1970s. Its origin came about after he observed how an artist gets lost in the making of their work to the extent they forget to eat and lose track of time. The research attempts to understand this phenomenon of *'intrinsic motivation'*, otherwise known as *'optimal experience'* or *'autotelic activity'* (auto = self, telos = goal). These labels try to describe an activity that is particular because *'it is rewarding in and of itself regardless of extrinsic rewards that might result from the activity'* (Csikszentmihalyi and Nakamura, 2009, p 195).

Csikszentmihalyi investigated the nature of intrinsic motivation by interviewing chess players, rock climbers, dancers, and others. Data has also been collected using the Experience Sampling Method (ESM) that he developed. With this, over 2000 people have been tracked by rating their daily states of consciousness on various numerical scales when prompted within two-hour periods by a random signal from a pager or watch. The data produces a *'virtual filmstrip of a person's daily activities and experiences'* (Csikszentmihalyi, 1997, p 46).

Findings from the research reveal that flow moments are likely to occur when activities incorporate two aspects. First, when activities have goals that are guided to some extent by rules that grant clarity of purpose, thus providing immediate feedback on how far the objective/s have been met, while at the same time affording flexibility of how goals are reached. Second, flow happens when a person is trying to tackle a challenge that their skills are just about capable of achieving, but where one can see where new learning is needed to achieve more.

> *The state is one of dynamic equilibrium ... The balance is fragile. If challenges exceed skills, one first becomes vigilant and then anxious; if skills exceed challenges, one first relaxes and eventually becomes bored. ... Shifts in the subjective state provide feedback about the changing relationship to the environment. Anxiety of boredom presses a person to adjust his or her level of skill and/or challenge, in order to escape the aversive state and reenter flow.*
> (Csikszentmihalyi and Nakamura, 2009, p 196)

Analysis of data suggests that the quality of an experience can be understood as a ratio between perceived challenges and skills. The ratio explains why many people reported having flow moments at work, and why some activities people do in their free time, away from work, are more rewarding in terms of flow than others. Also demonstrated in the research is that arriving at and maintaining flow requires personal investment. In other words, you need to have enough understanding about the goals and the rules of an activity to access it properly, plus you need to be prepared to push yourself if you want to experience flow. This line of reasoning supports Boden's argument about why learning rules is important when balanced with affording scope for creative thinking.

Csikszentmihalyi explains that for many people *'free time is more difficult to enjoy than work'* because *'our nervous system has evolved to attend to external signals, but has not had time to adapt to long periods without obstacles and dangers'*. He suggests that *'unless one learns how to use this time effectively, having leisure at one's disposal does not improve the quality of life'* (1997, p 48). He recommends that we find activities which necessitate devoting *'ingenuity and attention'* to, proposing this is why many of the treasures displayed in our museums exist and why we can listen to brilliant music. These result from *'people striving to express their best skill'* often *'in the time left free from work ... and chores'*. He adds:

> Only lack of imagination, or lack of energy, stand in the way of each of us becoming a poet or a musician, an inventor or explorer, an amateur scholar, scientist, artist, or collector.

> (Csikszentmihalyi, 1997, p 70)

The principles of the theory make it easy to see how sport can provide flow experiences. To join in with a sport a person needs to know the rules of the game; personal or team goals can be set; and to achieve goals takes time, energy and sometimes money. These need to be invested. Sports people participating in the Olympic games would attest to this, as would members of a successful regional youth football team. Other games, such as card games, chess or digital gaming spaces, also offer potential flow experiences for the same reasons.

Investing in relationships is something Csikszentmihalyi points to as being likely ground for flow experiences to occur. He uses the example of parenting, talking about people mentally investing in conversations with and about their children; attention is paid working towards common goals. With friends, pupils and colleagues too, successful interactions depend on finding out about what someone likes and might be interested in, allowing this to shape conversations and action. Dewey's (1938) description of *'co-operative enterprise'* in the classroom (discussed at the beginning of this chapter) resonates here, where a teacher is *'intelligently aware of the capacities, needs and past experiences of those under instruction'* (p 72) and where suggestions by all involved lead to further suggestions and the development of a plan. Csikszentmihalyi says that

> a good conversation is like a jam session in jazz, where one starts with conventional elements and then introduces spontaneous variations that create an exciting new composition.

He calls the collaborative nature of these experiences *'social flow'* (Csikszentmihalyi, 1997, 70). They have the added benefit of encouraging individuals to structure their thoughts so as to be understood. Consequently, he tells us, social flow acts as an impetus to sharpen communication skills.

Other flow experiences, such as going to a rugby match, or visiting an exhibition, or enjoying a theatre production can include social flow moments. To really enjoy these occasions, you need to invest time in learning the rules of play, or the artist's oeuvre, or a plot line, and conversations had with people you go with, interpreting what you have witnessed together, is part of the joy.

Csikszentmihalyi's research suggests that watching television is less likely to bring about flow moments because it is more passive, requiring less attention/investment. However, what do you think about this? Do you think it depends on what someone is watching and who with? How different is watching a sports fixture in a stadium than on television with like-minded friends who enjoy analysing the game? Can being absorbed in watching a film with a complex plot be considered a flow experience? If so, would it make a difference if it was seen in the cinema or on a television? Does the size of the television matter!? Is perhaps reading the book the film is based on potentially a more immersive flow experience? If so, why? These questions require us to think about how we construct personal meaning. We will return to these thoughts in Chapter 6.

Csikszentmihalyi's research undoubtedly provides a useful perspective on why it is important for teachers, and those who care for children at home, to open up a wide range of experiences for individuals to try out or at least be aware of. The hope is that children will gravitate towards things that could make a huge difference to how they spend their time, in or outside of school (or work when they are older), which might improve their quality of life. When Malorie Blackman's mother took her to their local library, and when Julia Donaldson and Toby Thompson's parents played music in the house, and when Patrick Brill and Andrew Marr's parents chatted openly about art and took them to art exhibitions, these introductions all made strong impressions that lasted a lifetime.

Claxton's theory of hare brain, tortoise mind thinking

When comedian John Cleese read a book by Guy Claxton, professor of learning sciences, titled *Hare Brain, Tortoise Mind: Why Intelligence Increases When You Think Less* (1998) it made a great deal of sense to him. The metaphors 'hare brain' and 'tortoise mind' – the first referring to how we think deliberately in a logical and purposeful way, the second alluding to when we think less rigorously in a more leisurely, musing manner – illuminated for John Cleese why he found certain conditions needed to be in place before his creativity began to flow (so he presumably could be in flow). As John Cleese writes in his book *Creativity: A Short and Cheerful Guide* (2020), these conditions contrasted with how he was taught to learn at school:

> The schools I attended concentrated entirely on teaching us to think logically, analytically and verbally … but what they didn't tell me was that while this way of thinking is absolutely right for solving certain kinds of problems, it's no good at all for other kinds.
>
> (Cleese, 2020, p 33)

He goes on to talk about how his own method of working when writing involves creating 'boundaries of space to stop others interrupting' (p 49). He says, 'The greatest killer of *creativity is interruption'*. External interruptions, like someone wanting to ask you something, or being distracted by an email or phone message popping up, *'pulls your mind away from what you want to be thinking about'* (p.46). This also happens with internal interruptions, such as thinking about something you have forgotten to do. He advises setting *'a specific play period that starts in a few minutes time and finishes, say, ninety minutes later'*.

> *You treat those ninety minutes with huge respect and don't allow any interruptions. And, knowing that this chunk of time is sacred, you can start to play ... You become aware of something you don't notice when you're dashing around – and that is that your head is full of silly little thoughts and worries ... people who are stronger-minded than me seem to be able to just bat these thoughts away. Lucky sods. I can't do that. Instead, I write them down straight away on a yellow sticky note ... then I can forget about them. Once you start chasing away any distracting thoughts, you'll discover, just like in meditation, that the longer you sit there, the more your mind slows and calms down and settles.*
>
> (Cleese, 2020, pp 50–53)

John Cleese is describing here the same playful, mind wandering, unstructured, yet serious, nature of creativity that other creative people in Chapter 1 remark on, and how it takes concentrated effort to achieve being in that mental space. For instance, Andrew Marr sees time alone with his canvas and oil paints in the open air as *'a test of spirit, self-belief and of determination'* (2013, p 19). Anish Kapoor talks about having *'the courage to sit in an empty studio'* and to *'dare'* to *'try some daft ideas out'*. Indeed, because time to experiment and play is viewed as so important by the creative people featured in Part 1 of this book, it is one of the three conditions identified as being crucial for nurturing creativity.

Claxton (1998) proposes with his hare brain, tortoise mind theory that for our mental capacities to be fully engaged both of these types of thinking (logical/purposeful; and leisurely/musing) need to be employed in an iterative way, and both should be valued equally. He tells us we need to shift from one type of thinking to the other, to and fro, coming up with lots of intuitive ideas (including some wacky ones) to solve a problem; followed by testing these rationally, narrowing down the ones that might logically work; then, going backwards and forwards again between hare and tortoise modes of thinking to search for an elegant solution that is interesting and original, and which works in the real world, and is therefore of real value. This process is Claxton's recipe for creative thinking, and it echoes the aesthetic cognitive constructivist conditions described by Dewey (1934) where he says in our attempt to satisfy our curiosity about what we see around us *'equilibrium comes about not mechanically and inertly but out of, and because of, tension'* (p 13). The process *'is not stagnation but is rhythmic and developing'* (p 18). In other words, it could be said that the tension between Claxton's hare brain and tortoise mind thinking modes is what creates the right conditions for creativity. Indeed, Passarelli and Kolb (2012), drawing on the work of Dewey, use the label *'creative tension'* (p 72). In Claxton's theory the tension is explained as reliant on how long a person can stand being in a state of uncertainty while experimenting with ideas (afforded by the tortoise mindset), rather than in a position of more rational thought. Without being open to new possibilities nothing new can happen, but uncertainty is risky; you have no idea when, or if, a problem will be successfully resolved. But risk is part of being creative.

We have seen that Craft (2001) refers to risk as one of the qualities necessary for little c creativity to take place. I see risk as part of our second identified condition for nurturing creativity, that of having time for experimentation and play. I am reminded here of a conversation I had with a group of primary school teacher training students with Toby Thompson about his creative process. He told us that even the week before performing a new show he would still be writing it, not quite knowing if everything would fit into place. That degree of risk many people might find intolerable, but the tension (between logical and musing mindsets) works very well for Toby.

Claxton believes one of the major problems in our everyday lives is the speed at which we are expected to make decisions. He deems this to be especially true in schools. He asks why thinking time tends to occur in pressurised atmospheres, hypothesising whether the urgency is designed to motivate, or alternatively is there a fear that drifting off task might mean wasting time. '*Slow*', he says, '*tends to be a euphemism for stupid*': '*Slow on the uptake*'. While '*quick wits*' are seen as better (Claxton, 2001, p 31). But, he points out, '*haring about*' and having '*hare brained ideas*' *(p 32)* is not helpful either. Hence, by comparing an aspect of human behaviour to having a hare brain – logical and purposeful, but fast and consequently not necessarily accurate and possibly missing the wider picture through lack of time pondering – the virtues of having a slower tortoise mindset becomes more apparent.

Claxton explains when hare brain thinking, all relevant information needs to be available to be analysed if accurate judgements are to be made. But, what happens if some information is missing? Where do we look for answers then? This is where tortoise mind thinking comes into play, and where, again, Dewey (1938) can also help us with these thoughts. You might remember from Dewey's description of his experiential continuum model the man who sees a prime piece of land who wants to build a house on it. After stopping and looking at the challenge, he needed to understand the significance of what he could see by reflecting on his past experiences in order to form a judgement of what to expect. This '*complex intellectual operation*' (p 69) (forming part of the '*plan*' (p 71) stage) allows him to have '*foresight of the consequences which will result from acting upon the impulse*' (p 68) to build the house. This process requires a wide perspective, enabled by years of looking and listening ie an accumulation of experiences. It is the same '*wisdom*' (p 38) Dewey talks about that adults need to exercise when teaching children (importantly, without imposing it). It is the wisdom that means the man can create a house that is uniquely his. And he needs both hare brain and tortoise mind thinking skills to do it.

Claxton (2001) tells us that this iterative wisdom (between both modes of thinking) does not necessarily lend itself to be put into words. He says, '*Forcing people to articulate and justify their reasons for making a decision may be tantamount to forcing them to neglect non-verbal data*' (p. 37). Here, Claxton refers to the intuitive gut-feeling style of tortoise mind thinking. His point reminds me of when a colleague of mine told me about taking some sixth-form students to talk to the artist Ron Mueck, who at the time had a studio in the basement of the National Gallery. A student asked what it was that Ron was trying to communicate in one of his sculptures. The response from the artist was that if he could say it in words, then he probably would not have made the sculpture. I found this reply interesting as it revealed the artist's need to express himself in a way that he felt he could do so most precisely. There is clearly a connection here with how Vygotsky explains how we take control over sociocultural psychological devices such as language, signs and symbols, and art – firstly on a *'social level'* (*'interpsychological'*) and then on an *'individual level'* (*'intrapsychological'*) (1978, p 57) (as already described in this chapter). Ron Mueck, in a highly sophisticated way, had taken personal control over the meaning of the imagery he created, but did not feel the same degree of ownership over spoken language. The student was keen to access the artist's meaning of the imagery, but instead had to rely on their own capacity to construct personal meaning using the same sociocultural process.

Claxton and Vygotsky's theories in this area assist our understanding of why some people who are experts in their field might not necessarily be best placed to teach others about what they do. In my own research (Hosack Janes, 2021), I have found that teachers with art expertise, or who have access to visiting artistic practitioners in a school, tend not to use teaching methods that replicate how artists experiment and play with ideas and materials (a process-driven approach). Instead, my findings show that teachers with art expertise (or access to it) are more likely to teach their subject using step-by-step instructions (a product-driven approach). This approach (as previously discussed) limits pupils' input into their own work and thus curtails their personal creative development. Also, remember what Boden said about the need for a balance between direct instruction and time allowed for experimentation and play where she gives advice on how not to *'smother'* creativity (2001, p 98). Regularly reflecting deeply on one's expert practice would help in correcting this problem, albeit also being aware of issues articulating *'non-verbal data'* (Claxton, 2001, p 37). However, it is also true that direct instruction makes the whole process of teaching less risky, and this might be the rationale for teachers using product-driven, step-by-step practices. But the appropriateness of such methods should be carefully considered in terms of learning objectives ie if a teacher's intention is to help nurture pupils' creative development they should question if this is the most effective approach. Risk, after all, as we have discussed, is part of the creative process.

Claxton, particularly in his work with teachers, promotes the importance of not undermining our intuitive, slow burning capacity to solve problems. Alongside other academics he supports the term *'thinking dispositions'* (Claxton, Costa and Kallick, 2016, p 63) to make clear that there are different ways of thinking that *'are crucial to a person's success in school and life'*. These include, for example, *'thinking flexibly'*, *'thinking independently'*, *'drawing on past knowledge'* and *'striving for accuracy'*. The overall aim is that *'a person becomes disposed* [or *'inclined'* is a word Claxton also uses (2021, p 80)] *to use a particular facet of practical intelligence'* so the *'disposition can grow and become more sophisticated'* (p 63). Just as Craft's (2001) concept of little c creativity was developed to help determine how children can become more self-directed in their learning, Claxton sees *'dispositions'* as a *'broad toolkit'* to increase *'independent thought and determination'* (2021, p 78).

It is important to point out here that the aim to increase independence is not the same as an ambition for a learner to be fully independent. That goal would be at odds with an understanding that guided learning benefits all learners. In a mutually respectful teacher–pupil relationship everyone brings their own abilities and experiences. This is key to appreciating knowledge as socially constructed, portrayed in a number of ways by the theorists in this chapter. For example, it is demonstrated in Dewey's '*co-operative enterprise*' (1938, p 72), Csikszentmihalyi's idea of '*social flow*' (1997, p 70) and Craft's (2001) recommendation to support learners in identifying and solving problems with prompting 'what if?' questions.

Claxton acknowledges in his book *The Future of Teaching: And the Myths That Hold It Back* (2021) that some teaching approaches which aim to assist pupils with developing skills to help them learn (often called Learning to Learn (L2L) strategies) have little or no impact because they are '*accompanied by a tick-box mentality*' (p 78). He tells us the emphasis needs to be on '*developing ... over time ... dispositions*' (also called in the book habits of mind, attributes and mindsets) that '*grow in strength, complexity and breadth of application*'. He recommends creating a common culture in a school to ensure dispositions/habits of mind/attributes/mindsets can be embedded across lessons. This includes agreeing on a common language with which to speak about these. He goes on to list examples of school chains and academics who are adding to a growing database of evidence for '*this fourth generation of thinking about L2L*' (p 78), and includes his own research, called Building Learning Power (BLP), and research from Harvard University's long-established Project Zero. We will look at one of the Project Zero projects in Chapter 5.

To conclude

I am tempted to conclude this chapter by summing up more than I have already key ideas in the theories that we have been examining. This is, however, something I am going to resist because it would reduce further my précised representations of some complex concepts. I will also avoid, for the same reason, trying to produce a list of main aspects that draw together the theories. This would be a very blunt instrument as each theory brings something different – a different perspective – to our exploration on how best to nurture creativity.

I have already cross-referenced many of the points made by the academics, and also with the experiences shared by the creative people in Part 1, and with my own research findings and experiences. With respect to the three conditions for nurturing creativity – valuing the arts in everyday life, having time to experiment and play, and opportunities to collaborate with others – all three, I believe, hold true under examination within the theories as agreeable conditions.

There are most likely (I hope) links you have also made between the theories in this chapter and your own experiences. Below are questions for you to reflect on aimed at prompting these further.

REFLECTIVE POINTS

- Having read about each of the theories in this chapter, are there any that particularly resonate with you?

- Are there other educational theories that you know about which you think support, or alternatively can be used to contest, the conditions for nurturing creativity identified in Part 1?

- Craft's thoughts on digital cultural spaces and possibility thinking (PT) view the child as 'capable and potent' rather than 'vulnerable and at risk' (2013, p 129). What are your thoughts on the potential of an online environment for nurturing creativity?

- Do you ever get so involved in an activity that you lose track of time? If so, when was the last time this happened? Do you consider what you were doing as your flow space, as described by Csikszentmihalyi?

Further reading

Claxton, G (2021) *The Future of Teaching and the Myths that Hold it Back*. Abingdon: Routledge.

Daniels, H (2016) *Vygotsky and Pedagogy*. Abingdon: Routledge.

Hosack Janes, K (2021) Objects of Curiosity: How Old Master Paintings Have Been Used in the Primary Classroom to Provide Pupils with Cognitive Challenge and Creative Agency. *Thinking Skills and Creativity*, 41.

References

Bakhshi, H, Frey, C and Osborne, M (2015) Creativity Vs. Robots: The Creative Economy and the Future of Employment. [online] Available at: https://media.nesta.org.uk/documents/creativity_vs._robots_wv.pdf (accessed 28 October 2021).

Boden, M (2001) Creativity and Knowledge, in Craft, A, Jeffrey, B and Liebling, M (eds) *Creativity in Education*. London: Continuum, pp 95–102.

Boden, M (2010) *Creativity and Art: Three Roads to Surprise*. Oxford: Oxford University Press.

Claxton, G (1998) *Hare Brain, Tortoise Mind: Why Intelligence Increases When You Think Less*. London: Fourth Estate.

Claxton, G (2001) The Innovative Mind: Becoming Smarter by Thinking Less, in Henry, J (ed) *Creative Management*. London: Sage.

Claxton, G (2021) *The Future of Teaching and the Myths that Hold it Back*. Abingdon: Routledge.

Claxton, G, Costa, A L and Kallick, B (2016) Hard Thinking about Soft Skills. *Educational Leadership*, 73 (6): 60–64.

Cleese, J (2020) *Creativity: A Short and Cheerful Guide*. London: Penguin, Random House.

Craft, A (2000) *Creativity across the Primary Curriculum: Framing and Developing Practice*. London: Routledge.

Craft, A (2001) Little c Creativity, in Craft, A, Jeffrey, B and Liebling, M (eds) *Creativity in Education*. London: Continuum, pp 45–61.

Craft, A (2002) *Creativity and Early Years Education*. London: Continuum.

Craft, A (2013) Childhood, Possibility Thinking and Wise, Humanising Educational Futures. *International Journal of Educational Research*, 61: 126–34.

Craft, A and Chappell, K (2014) Possibility Thinking and Social Change in Primary Schools. *Education 3-13*, 44 (4): 407–25.

Cremin, T, Burnard, P and Craft, A (2006) Pedagogy and Possibility Thinking in the Early Years. *Thinking Skills and Creativity*, 1 (2): 108–19.

Csikszentmihalyi, M (1990) *The Psychology of Optimal Experience*. New York: HarperCollins.

Csikszentmihalyi, M (1997) Finding Flow. *Psychology Today*, 30, 4; Health Research Premium Collection.

Csikszentmihalyi, M and Nakamura, J (2009) Flow Theory and Research, in Lopez, S J and Snyder, C R (eds) *The Oxford Handbook of Positive Psychology – Second Edition*. Oxford: Oxford University Press.

Daniels, H (2016) *Vygotsky and Pedagogy*. Abingdon: Routledge.

Dewey, J (1934) *Art as Experience*. New York: The Berkley Publishing Group.

Dewey, J (1938) *Experience and Education*. New York: Touchstone (first Touchstone edition published 1997).

Engeström, Y (1999) Innovative Learning in Work Teams: Analysing Cycles of Knowledge Creation in Practice, in Engeström, Y, Miettinen, R and Punamaki, R L (eds) *Perspectives on Activity Theory*. Cambridge: Cambridge University Press.

Engeström, Y (2012) The Historical-Cultural Activity Theory and Its Contributions to Education, Health and Communications: Interview with Yrjö Engeström by Monica Lemos. [online] Available at: https://marxismocritico .com/2013/11/08/the-historical-cultural-activity-theory-and-its-contributions-to-education-health-and -communication/ (accessed 1 July 2021).

Gardner, H (1993, reprint 2011) *Creating Minds: An Anatomy of Creativity Seen through the Lives of Freud, Einstein, Picasso, Stravinsky, Eliot, Graham, and Gandhi*. New York: Basic Books.

Hosack Janes, K (2014) *Using the Visual Arts for Cross-Curricular Teaching and Learning*. Abingdon: Routledge.

Hosack Janes, K (2021) Objects of Curiosity: How Old Master Paintings Have Been Used in the Primary Classroom to Provide Pupils with Cognitive Challenge and Creative Agency. *Thinking Skills and Creativity*, 41.

Hua Liu, C and Mathews, R (2005) Vygotsky's Philosophy: Constructivism and Its Criticisms Examined. *International Education Journal*, 6 (3): 386–99.

Kaufman, J C and Beghetto, R A (2009) Beyond Big and Little: The Four C Model of Creativity. *Review of General Psychology*, 13 (1): 1–12.

Marr, A (2013) *A Short Book about Drawing*. London: Quadrille Publishing Ltd.

Passarelli, A M and Kolb, D A (2012) The Learning Way: Learning from Experience as the Path to Lifelong Learning and Development, in London, M (ed) *The Oxford Handbook of Lifelong Learning*. Oxford: Oxford University Press.

Robinson, K (2006) Do Schools Kill Creativity? *TED Talk*. [online] Available at: https://www.ted.com/talks/sir_ken _robinson_do_schools_kill_creativity?language=en (accessed 3 February 2021).

Robinson, K (2009) *The Element: How Finding Your Passion Changes Everything*. London: Penguin Books.

Rusbridger, A (2020) *News and How to Use It: What to Believe in a Fake News World*. Edinburgh: Canongate Books Ltd.

Smith, B R (2020) *You Are an Artist*. London: Thames and Hudson Ltd.

Vygotsky, L S (trans.) (1978) *Mind in Society: The Development of Higher Psychological Processes*, Cole, M, John-Steiner, S, Scribner, S and Souberman, E (eds and trans). Cambridge, MA: Harvard University Press.

Vygotsky, L S (trans.) (1987) *The Collected Works of L.S. Vygotsky. Vol 1: Problems of General Psychology (including the volume Thinking and Speech)*, Rieber, R W and Carton, A S (eds), Minick, N (trans.). New York: Plenum Press.

Vygotsky, L S (trans.) (2004) Sharpe, M.E. (trans.). Imagination and Creativity in Childhood. *Journal of Russian and East European Psychology*, 42 (1): 7–97.

4 Finding consensus about creativity across educational frameworks

In this chapter we are going to continue to examine consensus around what creative conditions look like, this time focusing on some of the wide variety of advice and information published in different forms about creativity in educational settings.

To recap briefly on some of the publications mentioned in the Introduction chapter. In 1999, the National Advisory Committee on Creative and Cultural Education was tasked with taking stock of the provision available for the creative and cultural development of young people in the UK 'and to make proposals for principles, policies and practice' (1999, p 2). The final report framed creativity as promoting "the freedom to innovate and take risks' (p 10), that 'creativity always involves originality', and 'historic originality' is 'more likely to emerge from a system which encourages the creative capacities of everyone' (p 32). We also discussed in the Introduction chapter that the report's definition of creativity ('Imaginative activity fashioned so as to produce outcomes that are both original and of value', p 30) was subsequently cited in a number of UK government initiatives, policies and reports (for example, CCE, 2007, 2009, 2012; DfES, 2003; MLA, 2005; Ofsted, 2010; QCA, 2004). One of these was a set of non-statutory guidance notes for teachers, titled Creativity: Find It, Promote It (QCA, 2004). This publication called the 'characteristics of creativity': 'Imagination and purpose', 'Originality' and 'Value' (p 7) (ie directly taken from the NACCCE definition). This teachers' resource went on to say that 'creativity improves pupils' self-esteem, motivation and achievement' by making pupils

> more interested in discovering things for themselves; more open to new ideas; keen to work with others; and willing to work beyond lesson time when pursuing an idea or vision.
>
> (p 9)

Teachers are told they are

> *likely to see pupils being creative if they see them questioning and challenging; making connections and seeking relationships; envisioning what might be; exploring ideas; and reflecting critically on ideas, actions and outcomes.*

(p 10)

We also discussed in the Introduction chapter that there are real difficulties in pinning down creativity, particularly when it comes to gathering data on its impact. We looked at that fact that, according to several international meta-analyses (Winner and Hetland, 2000; See and Kokotsaki, 2017; Cremin and Chappell, 2019), current empirical evidence on creative pedagogies – about what they are and what they do – is lacking or inconsistent. Nevertheless, we also heard that common themes can be found. Cremin and Chappell (2019) propose '*seven interrelating features of creative pedagogy*': '*Risk-taking*', '*encouraging autonomy and agency*', '*generating and exploring ideas*', '*playfulness*', '*problem-solving*', '*co-constructing and collaborating*' and '*teacher creativity*' (p 13).

The difference in how the NACCCE (1999) and QCA (2004) documents recount the subject of creativity, as opposed to how Winner and Hetland (2000), See and Kokotsaki (2017) and Cremin and Chappell (2019) communicate their findings, is important. Although similar in content, the advocacy in the NACCCE and QCA publications requires support from empirical data. In contrast, the authors of the meta-analyses acknowledge that there is a dearth of evidence in this area, though common themes can be seen.

It is apparent in these different forms of information and advice about creativity in education that many of the words and phrases used are the same or plainly relate to each other. This also applies to the words and phrases used in the Durham Commission's three separate definitions of '*creativity*', '*creative thinking*' and '*teaching for creativity*' (2019, p 96) (see the Introduction chapter for these). Variations on words, such as 'original'/'originality', 'individual'/'individuality' and 'imagination'/'imaginative' appear across documents. The words 'exploring' and 'experimenting' seem interchangeable, particularly when coupled with the word 'ideas'. And 'working together' and 'collaborating'/'collaborative' are clearly the same. In addition, words like '*questioning*' (QCA, 2004, p 10), '*playfulness*', '*agency*', '*co-construction*' (Cremin and Chappell, 2019, p 13) and '*perseverance*' (Durham Commission, 2019, p 96) are reminiscent of the language used in some of the theoretical frameworks examined in the last chapter. This also applies to phrases such as '*historic originality*' (NACCCE, 1999, p 32) and '*envisioning what might be*' (QCA, 2004, 10).

Creative conditions and creative outcomes

For the purposes of this book we want to consider how most effectively conditions can be cultivated for creativity to flourish. This means being clear about what constitutes a creative condition, and what would be more fittingly termed as a creative outcome. For example, 'exploring ideas' and 'collaborating' are conditions. These need to be put in place for creativity to be nurtured, consequently we have already identified both throughout the course of the book as conditions for nurturing creativity; namely having time for experimentation and play, and providing opportunities to collaborate with others. You will remember that these two conditions are evident in the recollections of the creative people featured in Chapter 1. On the other hand, 'originality', 'individuality' and 'imagination' can most usefully be understood and classified as outcomes. The aim is that these will result from an activity which has been planned with creative conditions in mind.

Let us now look at some more published advice and information on creativity, taking particular note of what might be classified as creative conditions for nurturing creativity, or more appropriately termed as creative outcomes. In addition, let us consider whether any conditions set out as requirements or recommendations in the following examples might lead to the creative outcomes described. We will start by looking at the structure of some examples of curricular frameworks that expressly aim to support creativity.

Curricular framework examples

In England, in 2008 a statutory framework to be used by all early years providers for children under the age of five was introduced (DCSF, 2008). Called the Early Years Foundation Stage (EYFS) framework, it set out six '*Early learning goals and educational programmes*', one of which was '*Creative development*'. It states:

> Children's creativity must be extended by the provision of support for their curiosity, exploration and play. They must be provided with opportunities to explore and share their thoughts, ideas and feelings, for example, through a variety of art, music, movement, dance, imaginative and role-play activities, mathematics and design and technology.
>
> (DCSF, 2008, p 15)

When the framework was updated (DfE, 2017; DfE, 2021) it was structured differently to contain seven '*inter-connected*' '*Areas of learning and development*'. These are: '*Communication and language*', '*Physical development*', '*Personal, social and emotional development*', '*Literacy*', '*Mathematics*', '*Understanding the world*' and '*Expressive arts and design*' (p 7). The first three areas are stated as being '*particularly important for building a foundation for igniting children's curiosity and enthusiasm for learning, forming relationships and thriving*' (p 8).

In the revised version of the framework, teachers are told that their planning should be guided by '*three characteristics of effective teaching and learning*', stated as:

> Playing and exploring – children investigate and experience things, and 'have a go'
>
> Active learning – children concentrate and keep on trying if they encounter difficulties, and enjoy achievements
>
> Creating and thinking critically – children have and develop their own ideas, make links between ideas, and develop strategies for doing things
>
> (DfE, 2021, p 16)

Clearly the characteristic 'Playing and exploring' relates to the experiment and play condition for nurturing creativity that we have been discussing in this book. Also, the 'Active learning' characteristic would be recognised by Craft and Claxton (see the previous chapter for theorist references) as an articulation of risk-taking. And Craft and Boden would no doubt understand 'investigate and experience' and for children to 'develop their own ideas' as conditions for encouraging everyday creativity.

Valuing the arts in everyday life – our first condition for nurturing creativity – is encouraged in each version of the EYFS framework; the original having the arts included as one of the six learning areas, namely 'Creative development' (described above); and the updated framework has an 'Expressive arts and design' area of learning, stating:

> The development of children's artistic and cultural awareness supports their imagination and creativity. It is important that children have regular opportunities to engage with the arts, enabling them to explore and play with a wide range of media and materials. The quality and variety of what children see, hear and participate in is crucial for developing their understanding, self-expression, vocabulary and ability to communicate through the arts. The frequency, repetition and depth of their experiences are fundamental to their progress in interpreting and appreciating what they hear, respond to and observe.
>
> (DfE, 2021, p 10)

The 'Early learning goals' for the 'Expressive arts and design' area of learning are set out as two aspects:

> Creating with materials – Children at the expected level of development will:
>
> - Safely use and explore a variety of materials, tools and techniques, experimenting with colour, design, texture, form and function
> - Share their creations, explaining the process they have used
> - Make use of props and materials when role playing characters in narratives and stories
>
> Being Imaginative and Expressive – Children at the expected level of development will:
>
> - Invent, adapt and recount narratives and stories with peers and their teacher
> - Sing a range of well-known nursery rhymes and songs
> - Perform songs, rhymes, poems and stories with others, and when appropriate try to move in time with music
>
> (DfE, 2021, p 15)

The emphasis in the EYFS frameworks on the absence of artificial barriers between subject areas (an approach often known as a cross-curricular or thematic) allows teachers the flexibility to use the arts for teaching and learning many subjects.

Neither version of the framework specifies which artistic and cultural examples children are required to be exposed to. This is left to the discretion of teachers. Generally, this is also the case in the national curriculum in England for pupils aged between 5 and 16 (DfE, 2014) where teachers are given free rein to make choices about which contexts for learning they use ie which stimuli and themes they teach subject area '*Programmes of study*' through. Schools, however, '*must offer a curriculum which is balanced and broadly based and which promotes the spiritual, moral, cultural, mental and physical development of pupils*' (DfE, 2014, p 2.1). How a school manages to plan for this is assessed when a judgement is made by the Office for Standards in Education (Ofsted) about the quality of education in a school. '*Inspectors will consider the extent to which schools are equipping pupils with the knowledge and cultural capital they need to succeed in life*' (Ofsted, 2021, p 204). Ofsted's understanding of '*cultural capital*' is

> *the essential knowledge that pupils need to be educated citizens, introducing them to the best that has been thought and said and helping to engender an appreciation of human creativity and achievement.*

This statement is taken directly from the national curriculum aims (DfE, 2014, p 3.1) and is intentionally broad to accommodate all subject areas and teachers' choices.

It is certainly true that stating at the national level a selection of artistic and cultural examples is fraught with complications. What to include, and what to leave out? In 2021, a non-statutory Model Music Curriculum (DfE, 2021a) was published in England which endeavoured to flesh out the minimal mandatory requirements of the national curriculum for music for pupils between 5 and 14 years old with advice on '*age-appropriate*' (p 13) music for each year group. Accompanying notes state:

> *Music is one of the central building blocks of any culture and the shared knowledge of music is crucial cultural capital in understanding where we come from and our place in the world. An inclusive approach to this cultural capital is represented in this document to encourage pupils to be open minded in their listening as well as knowledgeable about the breadth of musical genres in the world today.*
>
> *Teachers are encouraged to use pieces from a wide range of cultures and traditions that truly reflect the community in which they are teaching. The pieces in the following tables have been suggested ... to ensure that pupils gain a broad aural knowledge of Western Classical Music, Popular Music (broadly defined) and Traditional Music from around the world. Through active listening to these or equivalent works, many of which can be found in the Appendix ..., all pupils will be given a solid aural foundation that doesn't rely on previous musical exposure.*
>
> (DfE, 2021a, p 8)

Whether you are a music specialist or not, you are bound to have thoughts on what you might include in a chronological and inclusive list. It will depend, of course, on what you have already been exposed to yourself, and perhaps your preferences. And there lies one of the complications for creating such a canon: the perpetuation of the same usual suspects. However, for the non-specialists – especially – such lists can be extremely helpful, particularly if they are broad and for guidance only, and if teachers are encouraged to include our own choices, as the Model Music Curriculum recommends.

The Welsh national curriculum, published in 2020, is another example of a curricular framework that expressly states to support the creativity of pupils. It *'aims to help each school develop its own curriculum, enabling their learners to develop towards the four purposes of the curriculum'* (2020a). These *'four purposes'*, we are told, are *'a shared vision ... developed by practitioners through a network of schools'* (2020b). They are for every child and young person in Wales, aged between 3 and 16 years old, and *'should be the starting point and aspiration for schools' curriculum design'* (2020a). Schools are required to support learners to become:

1. *Ambitious, capable learners, ready to learn throughout their lives*

2. *Enterprising, creative contributors, ready to play a full part in life and work*

3. *Ethical, informed citizens of Wales and the world*

4. *Healthy, confident individuals, ready to lead fulfilling lives as valued members of society*

Curriculum for Wales (2020a)

The second purpose is expanded into a definition of what *'enterprising and creative contributors'* can do:

*   *Connect and apply their knowledge and skills to create ideas and products*

*   *Think creatively to reframe and solve problems*

*   *Identify and grasp opportunities*

*   *Take measured risks*

*   *Lead and play different roles in teams effectively and responsibly*

*   *Express ideas and emotions through different media*

*   *Give of their energy and skills so that other people will benefit*

Curriculum for Wales (2020a)

Teachers are told that the *'four purposes'* need to be *'underpinned'* with *'integral skills'*, which are:

> *Creativity and innovation – learners should be given space to be curious and inquisitive, and to generate many ideas. They should be supported to link and connect disparate experiences, knowledge and skills, and see, explore and justify alternative solutions.*

> *Critical thinking and problem-solving – learners should be supported to ask meaningful questions, and to evaluate information, evidence and situations. They should be able to analyse and justify possible solutions, recognising potential*

issues and problems. Learners should become objective in their decision-making, identifying and developing arguments. They should be able to propose solutions which generate different types of value [defined in the curriculum as 'worth and importance in a range of contexts, including financial, cultural, social and learning value'].

Personal effectiveness – learners should develop emotional intelligence and awareness, becoming confident and independent. They should have opportunities to lead debate and discussion, becoming aware of the social, cultural, ethical and legal implications of their arguments. They should be able to evaluate their learning and mistakes, identifying areas for development.

Planning and organising – where developmentally appropriate, learners should be able to set goals, make decisions … reflect and adapt, as well as manage time, people and resources … the development of these skills allows learners to work across disciplines, providing them with opportunities for both synthesis and analysis. There is particular potential for innovation in making and using connections between different disciplines and Areas.

Curriculum for Wales (2020a)

The 'Areas' referred to in the above statement are the six 'Areas of learning and experience': 'Expressive arts', 'Health and well-being', 'Humanities', 'Language, literacy and communication', 'Numeracy and mathematics' and 'Science and technology'.

Under the 'Expressive arts' area, 'gaining an understanding and an appreciation of cultures and societies in Wales and in the world' and 'exploring cultural differences through time and place' are a requirement. Like with the national curriculum for England, the choice of artistic and cultural examples is left to individual schools and their teachers to decide, although the work of a handful of artists that 'have a distinct relationship to Wales' are given as suggestions and a focus on Welsh culture and traditions is expected to be embedded in the design of a school's curriculum (described as a 'cross-cutting theme'). 'Experimentation' with 'resources, materials and techniques' is also stipulated in the 'Expressive arts' area, and the creative process is described as 'learners explore, respond to stimuli and create and reflect on their own work while engaging in rich authentic experiences', where 'authentic' is described as 'real life experiences and contexts'. Overall, it is clear that the Welsh national curriculum intentionally addresses valuing the arts and allowing time for experimentation and play.

When it comes to assessing pupil progression within the 'Expressive arts' area, the Welsh national curriculum has three 'what matters' 'descriptions of learning', each with increasingly sophisticated 'I can' statements. For example, the 'description of learning' for 'Exploring the expressive arts is essential for developing artistic skills and knowledge and it enables learners to become curious and creative individuals' has the following progression step 1 statements.

- *I can explore and experiment with a variety of creative techniques, materials, processes, resources, tools and technologies.*

- *I can ask questions to discover how creative work is made.*

- *I am beginning to explore ideas, feelings and moods in a variety of creative work.*

Progression step 2 for the same description of learning includes the following statements:

- *I can explore and experiment with and then select appropriate creative techniques, practices, materials, processes, resources, tools and technologies.*

- *I can explore how and why creative work is made by asking questions and developing my own answers.*

- *I can explore and describe how artists and creative work communicate mood, feelings and ideas.*

Progression step 3 statements are:

- *I can explore and experiment independently and demonstrate technical control with a range of creative materials, processes, resources, tools and technologies showing innovation and resilience.*

- *I can explore the effects that a range of creative techniques, materials, processes, resources, tools and technologies have on my own and others' creative work.*

- *I can explore how creative work can represent, document, share and celebrate personal, social and cultural identities.*

- *I can explore and describe how artists and creative work communicate mood, feelings and ideas and the impact they have on an audience.*

For progression step 4 the statements are:

- *I can explore and experiment with my own and others' creative ideas, demonstrating increasingly complex technical control, innovation, independent thinking and originality to develop my work with confidence, being able to explain my reasons behind choices made and evaluate their effectiveness on my creative work.*

- *I can explore creative work, understanding the personal, social, cultural and historical context, including the conventions of the period in which it was created.*

- *I can investigate and understand how meaning is communicated through the ideas of other artists and performers.*

And, finally, progression step 5 for the same description of learning statements are:

- *I can explore and experiment with my own creative ideas and those of others, demonstrating technical control, innovation, independent thinking and originality, showing confidence to take risks and developing resilience in order to overcome creative challenges.*

- *I can investigate and analyse how creative work is used to represent and celebrate personal, social and cultural identities.*

- *I can independently research the purpose and meaning of a wide range of creative work and consider how they can impact on different audiences.*

Curriculum for Wales (2020a)

Teachers are told that although it is recognised different pupils develop at different rates, the statements '*broadly relate to age*' (from 3 to 16 year-olds). However, I would question if the '*four purposes*' and '*integral skills*' (as previously listed) are fully reflected in the earlier progression steps, ie for the younger children. For instance, why is exploring cultural identity not mentioned until step 3? Why is an expectation for pupils to be original in their thinking and to explain reasons behind their choices not mentioned until step 4? These aspects are entirely appropriate for all age groups to engage in. Also, the word '*independent*' (step 3 '*experiment independently*', step 4 '*independent thinking*' and step 5 '*independently research*') seems to be at odds with a curriculum that is aiming to progressively deepen understanding. As we looked at in the previous chapter, it is important to distinguish aiming to increase learners' independence from an ambition for a learner to be fully independent, otherwise the constructivist notion of guided learning, favoured by the theorists in Chapter 3, is dismantled.

A final example of a curricular framework that explicitly aims to support pupils' creative development is the Reggio Emilia approach, founded by Loris Malaguzzi in Northern Italy in response to the devastation caused by the Second World War. The citizens of the small city of Reggio Emilia sought to empower their preschool children in a style of learning that would enable the community to positively move forward. The basic principle that drives teaching is that it is based on what the children want to learn. The schools have ateliers (art studios) as a characteristic feature (Malaguzzi, 1998) and use a documentation method for recording individual children's '*feelings; conversations and discussions; interactions and relationships; gesture, stance and posture*' (Thornton and Brunton, 2009, p 110). Children are encouraged to express themselves using '*a hundred languages*' (p 2) (I would wholeheartedly recommend reading Loris Malaguzzi's celebrated poem titled 'A Hundred Languages', translated by Lella Gandini, which explains the Reggio Emilia philosophy).

Learner outcomes are collected in photographs, videos, written notes, drawings, annotated charts and examples of children's work (in progress and completed). The work is then interpreted by an educator, who has '*refined and developed their skills of observation and interpretation over many years*' (p 112). In turn, these are shared and reinterpreted continually with the team of adults at the schools.

The approach has inspired many educators in a number of countries of different age groups, for example, a research project in the UK called 5×5×5=Creativity coordinated by Bath Spa University. The findings of one evaluation from this project (Edlers, 2017, p 3) are presented as brief descriptions of practice under the headings: '*Sharing and relationships*', '*Ownership of learning*', '*Contextualised learning*', '*Co-enquiry*', '*Balance of structure and freedom*' and '*Making learning visible*'. Revealed are ways of working that are not dissimilar to those described by Dewey (1938) where he talks about '*co-operative enterprise*' (p 72), although the role of the teacher seems more removed from the group, essentially observing and offering opportunities for exchanges to take place. Another evaluation (Fawcett and Hay, 2004) from the same Bath Spa University project reports that the process of documentation is very time consuming and requires significant practice from the participants to develop the necessary skills.

The conditions for nurturing creativity set out in the examples of curricular frameworks presented above emphasise process-led pedagogies, where learners (to a varying degree) are guided by educators, but at the same time are afforded space to explore their own personal meanings about the world they live in. In each example the arts play a key role.

Assessing creative development

In 2015, Guy Claxton (whose notion of hare brain, tortoise mind thinking we looked at in the last chapter), together with his colleague Bill Lucas, proposed in their book *Educating Ruby: What Our Children Really Need to Learn* a vision of a school curriculum focusing on '7Cs': '*Creativity*', '*Curiosity*', '*Collaboration*', '*Confidence*', '*Communication*', '*Commitment*' and '*Craftsmanship*' – the first three of which directly correspond to the conditions put forward in this book. Their idea came about following a conversation they had concerning the 1983 Willy Russell award-winning film *Educating Rita*. In it, the title character slowly develops confidence in her own abilities to think critically and to learn because of the respectful educational environment she finds herself belonging to. Claxton and Lucas, in their 7Cs proposal, update the scenario by imagining what Ruby, a fictional granddaughter of Rita's, requires from a school today to experience a similar positive education.

The 7Cs proposition led to research at the University of Winchester by Lucas and Spencer (2017) into a range of formative assessment methods intended to help teachers and students track the progression of creativity. We are told in one of the publications reporting on the research that the word '*track*' was '*deliberately used … to encourage those who might otherwise see assessment of creative thinking as undesirable*' (p 160). Let us unpack this issue now.

We have seen for ourselves in some of the examples of curricular frameworks in this chapter that documenting pupils' creative progress is not straightforward. The main problem can be summed up as those things that are easier to test are things that are easier to teach because they have more certain, definite answers. However, if something is easier to test, it is also easier to automate. And this crucial point takes us back to the economic arguments made by Bakhshi, Frey and Osbourne in their report *Creativity Vs Robots* (2015), discussed in the Introduction chapter, detailing why we need to educate pupils for the interpretive, creative and collaborative nature of jobs that are less likely to be computerised in the future. Craft (2012) offers the opinion that there is a disconnect between subjects that are easily assessed through tests and a lack of trust in flexible and imaginative pedagogical approaches to assessment. Lucas and Spencer (2017) suggest that '*practically speaking, if creative thinking is assessed it is likely to be easier for teachers to prioritise its inclusion in busy schools'* (p 159). We can therefore see from this discourse there is growing agreement that some kind of creative development assessment/tracking is needed. But, as we have also discussed in this book, there are real difficulties with methods for evidencing the impact of creativity (Winner and Hetland, 2000; See and Kokotsaki, 2017; Cremin and Chappell, 2019).

You might recall from the Introduction chapter that we considered the difference between measuring and assessing, where measurement is to do with descriptions of quantity, and assessment with appraising the value of something (Eisner, 2002). Divergent thinking tests, such as Torrance Tests of Creative Thinking (Torrance, 1966), attempt to measure creativity (therefore quantitatively) by scoring outcomes. For example, a score is arrived at for fluency by counting the number of ideas generated to a given stimulus. Originality is calculated by identifying within a sample which ideas are given less frequently. Runco and Acar (2012) conclude that divergency tests *'are good indicators of future creative performance ... but someone can do well on a test of divergent thinking and never actually perform in a creative fashion'* (p 66). This is because divergent thinking needs to be coupled with convergent thinking, where multiple ideas are evaluated and developed. In divergent thinking tests, by reducing creativity to measuring using numerical data the whole creative process is not under review. Richer information about creative development is offered by more qualitative formative assessment. This type of assessment provides the learner and teacher (and whoever else is interested) with the opportunity to reflect on the process in order to improve performance further.

Lucas and Spencer's (2017) research into formative assessment methods for creative thinking brings together what they call *'signature pedagogies'* (p 6) – a term borrowed from Lee Shulman (2005). *'The idea of signature pedagogies'*, we are told, *'are the teaching and learning methods which are most likely to lead to the desired capability'* (p 7). *'Capability'* is used here in the same way Claxton uses the word *'dispositions'* (2021, p 78), which are also known as habits of mind/attributes/mindsets (see Chapter 3). Lucas and Spencer propose five *'inter-connected'* signature pedagogies which consciously draw on the work of other academics in the field of creativity. Below I have placed next to the signature pedagogies the names of academics where they have been specifically acknowledged:

1. *Problem-based learning*

2. *Classroom learning community – Chris Watkins (2005) and work from University College London Institute of Education (IoE)*

3. *Playful experimentation*

4. *Growth mindset – Carol Dweck (2006)*

5. *Deliberate practice – K Anders Ericsson (2016)*

(Lucas and Spencer, 2017, p 37)

Lucas and Spencer tell us that these pedagogies are to be used in tandem with their own *'five-dimensional model of creative thinking'* that aims to encourage students and teachers to reflect on *'habits'*. Each of the five habits (below) are purposefully written as adjectives, divided again into *'sub-habits'* that are *'action phrases ... to ensure the concepts are well grounded'* (p 23).

Imagination – *Using intuition, Making connections, Playing with possibilities*

Inquisitive – *Wondering and questioning, Exploring and investigating, Challenging assumptions*

Persistent – *Tolerating uncertainty, Sticking with difficulty, Daring to be different*

Collaborative – *Sharing the product, Giving and receiving feedback, Cooperating appropriately*

Disciplined – *Reflecting critically, Developing techniques, Crafting and improving*

(Lucas and Spencer, 2017, p 22)

Many of these habits have already been discussed in this book. The *'Collaborative'* habit is one of our conditions for nurturing creativity. Also, patently, *'Playing with possibilities'* can be linked to the work of Craft (2000, 2001, 2002). *'Tolerating uncertainty'* is akin to the risk-taking Craft (2001), Claxton (1998) and the NACCCE (1999) focus in on. And the word *'daring'* would strike a chord with Anish Kapoor, and also with Andrew Marr and John Cleese (see Chapter 1). Personally, I would gather together *'Using intuition'*, *'Making connections'*, *'Playing with possibilities'*, *'Wondering and questioning'*, *'Exploring and investigating'*, *'Tolerating uncertainty'*, *'Sticking with difficulty'* and *'Daring to be different'* under the umbrella condition – time for experimentation and play. To some extent, if the activity includes input from the learner, rather than simply following instructions, I would also include *'Developing techniques'* and *'Crafting and improving'* within the time for experimentation and play condition. This grouping is not to suggest that I disagree with the more nuanced approach that Lucas and Spencer have taken. I am merely looking for consensus on what we collectively mean by helping pupils to develop their creativity. There is nothing in their model, I believe, that any of the theorists or creative people in this book would disagree with. Indeed, Lucas and Spencer have also drawn on others to find consensus.

In addition to the recommendation by Lucas and Spencer for pupils and teachers to use the five-dimensional model habits and sub-habits as reflection points (including an idea to gauge levels of confidence in each, from 'Beginning', through to 'Developing', 'Confident' and 'Expert'), they endorse a host of other assessment methods with which to triangulate creative progression over time. This involves approaches that would be familiar to higher education students and industry professionals, such as compiling portfolios (physical and digital), writing logs, and diaries and journals. They equally promote the idea of peer review and group crits, described by Julian Nott in Chapter 1 *'as exhilarating and exciting'* when speaking about his experiences at the National Film and Television School, and expert reviews and performance tasks, a practice that Toby Thompson in Chapter 1 referred to as *'authentic'* when talking about working with industry professionals at the Theatre Royal Bath.

The role of PISA data

The Programme for International Student Assessment (PISA) is a study run by the Organisation for Economic Co-operation and Development (OECD) into different education systems in more than 80 countries. Launched in 1997, every three years comparative data on the performance of 15-year-olds in reading, mathematics and science are collected through testing and questionnaires of in excess of half a million young people. In 2015 the research also explored '*Collaborative problem solving*', and in 2018 '*Global competence*'. Results are published on the OECD website and disseminated through global conferences.

Speaking at a Paris conference in 2020 focusing on *Boosting Creativity in Education*, Andreas Schleicher, Director of Education and Skills at OECD, talked about how it is possible to correlate teachers' enthusiasm with higher reading scores. This demonstrates, he explains, that learning is a '*relational phenomenon*' rather than a '*transitional*' one, saying that what you study in school has a lot to do with the teachers you meet and '*their personalities – whether they recognise your personality*'. He warns about '*squashing too much into a school curriculum*' because this can mean '*the beautiful features of the world become shallow shadows of themselves*'. He illustrates this with an example of ten-year-olds getting excited about scientific experiments, which are the '*essence of science*'; whereas 15-year-olds can get bored having to learn formulas and knowledge straight from books. He believes there needs to be more of a shift from prioritising content knowledge to epistemic knowledge because '*the modern world rewards you with what you can do with what you know*'. He goes on to suggest '*student co-operation*' and '*co-creation*' enable this change in emphasis, quoting statistics from the PISA publication 'Do students learn in co-operative or competitive environments?' (2020). '*Co-operative*' environments in this document are described as those '*in education, when students, teachers, parents and the school principal know and trust each other, work together, and share information, ideas and goals*' (p 2). This should not be confused with the specific way that Dewey describes a '*co-operative enterprise*' (1938, p 38) (see Chapter 3); however, the OECD description relays the same respectful, sociocultural shared experience advocated by all the theorists included in this book.

The findings from Likert scale responses from young people to a PISA questionnaire reveal that reading scores for 15-year-olds who indicated they were taught in a co-operative environment were higher than those indicating they were taught in a competitive one. Nevertheless, the picture is fairly mixed, as these four key statements demonstrate.

- *Student co-operation was most prevalent, relative to competition, in Austria, Croatia, The Czech Republic, Denmark, Georgia, Germany, Japan, the Netherlands and Switzerland, whereas student competition was most prevalent, relative to co-operation, in Brazil, Ireland, Korea, Malta, Morocco, Saudi Arabia, Singapore, the United Kingdom and the United States.*

- *On average across OECD countries, students felt more comfortable in co-operative than in competitive learning environments.*

- *A more competitive learning environment was more strongly associated with favourable non-academic outcomes amongst boys than amongst girls.*

- *Students who see themselves as competitive, especially those who say they try harder when in competition with others, scored higher in reading than students who perceived themselves as less competitive.*

(OECD, 2020, p 2)

It seems then that a balance between these pedagogic environments is needed, with the report concluding that the '*bottom line*' is:

Fruitful and positive learning environments promote co-operative behaviours, but also competitive ones, if only because competition can be thrilling and enjoyable, and a competitive spirit may improve academic performance. For instance, team competitions, which combine both co-operative and competitive behaviours, are exciting and rewarding for participants.

(OECD, 2020, p 5)

Results are due in 2024 from PISA tests examining for the first time 15-year-olds' '*capacities to generate diverse and original ideas, and to evaluate and improve ideas, across a range of contexts or "domains"*' (OECD, 2021). This test for '*Creative thinking*' has been devised by an expert panel including Bill Lucas, whose work we have just looked at in this chapter. The test requires students to '*engage with open tasks that have no single correct response*'. The '*domains*' being tested are: '*Written expression, visual expression, social problem solving* and *scientific problem solving*'. Scoring methods are based on rubrics informed by sample responses. Particularly regarding methodology, as well as the findings, the final report will make fascinating reading.

In the Introduction chapter, I mentioned the 2020 online conference *Education Disrupted* where 1173 participants voted overwhelmingly against '*testing*' as something that schools and systems should treat as central in post-pandemic planning. However, we have seen in this chapter how research data, including data collected from testing, can improve our awareness of young people's creative development and can be used to shape curricular design and assessment methods. Perhaps then it is useful to think about testing/assessing/tracking in terms of how it informs practice, both for the individual through formative assessment methods, and through data collection methods that can inform policymakers at school and government levels.

The following reflective points will help you to consider further your own position on the important issues covered in this chapter.

REFLECTIVE POINTS

- Critically review the specific details of a national curriculum area relevant to your own interests paying attention to how it describes conditions for learning as well as outcomes. To what extent and in what ways does it encourage creative development?

- Think about which specific artistic and cultural examples you would include in a curriculum to teach a particular age group of pupils about a subject area. Concentrate on including a wide range of examples from different periods and cultures, as well as how you might make links to other subject areas. Explain your rationale for your choices.

- Consider how useful you find the habits and sub-habits in Lucas and Spencer's (2017) five-dimensional model of creative thinking for planning creative activities. Are there aspects you would like to use, or adapt to use, in your own practice?

- What forms of assessment described in this chapter have you experienced from a learner's and/or teacher's perspective? Which have you found most useful in helping to improve creative outcomes?

Further reading

Lucas, B and Spencer, E (2017) *Teaching Creative Thinking: Developing Learners Who Generate Ideas and Can Think Critically*. Williston: Crown House Publishing.

Malaguzzi, L. A Hundred Languages (trans. Gandini, L) (n.d.). [online] Available at: https://www.reggiochildren.it/en/reggio-emilia-approach/100-linguaggi-en/ (accessed 2 September 2021).

References

Bakhshi, H, Frey, C and Osborne, M (2015) Creativity Vs. Robots: The Creative Economy and the Future of Employment. [online] Available at: https://media.nesta.org.uk/documents/creativity_vs._robots_wv.pdf (accessed 28 October 2021).

Claxton, G (1998) *Hare Brain, Tortoise Mind: Why Intelligence Increases When You Think Less*. London: Fourth Estate.

Claxton, G (2021) *The Future of Teaching and the Myths that Hold it Back*. Abingdon: Routledge.

Claxton, G and Lucas, B (2015) *Educating Ruby: What Our Children Really Need to Learn*. Carmarthen: Crown House Publishing.

Cleese, J (2020) *Creativity: A Short and Cheerful Guide*. London: Penguin, Random House.

Curriculum for Wales (2020a) *Curriculum for Wales Guidance*. Welsh Government. [online] Available at: https://hwb.gov.wales/curriculum-for-wales/introduction. (accessed 18 August 2021).

Curriculum for Wales (2020b) *Policy and Strategy.* Welsh Government. [online] Available at: https://gov.wales/ curriculum-wales-overview (accessed 18 August 2021).

Craft, A (2000) *Creativity across the Primary Curriculum: Framing and Developing Practice.* London: Routledge.

Craft, A (2001) Little c Creativity, in Craft, A, Jeffrey, B and Liebling, M (eds) *Creativity in Education.* London: Continuum, pp 45–61.

Craft, A (2002) *Creativity and Early Years Education.* London: Continuum.

Craft, A (2012) Childhood in a Digital Age: Creative Challenges for Educational Futures, in Coate, K and Boulos, A (eds) *Creativity in Education: Challenging the Assumptions. London Review of Education,* 10 (2): 173–190. London: UCL IOE Press.

Department for Children, Schools and Families (DCSF) (2008) *Statutory Framework for the Early Years Foundation Stage: Setting the Standards for Learning, Development and Care for Children from Birth to Five.* London: DCSF. [online] Available at: http://earlyyearsmatters.co.uk/wp-content/uploads/2011/01/Statutory-Framework-for-the -Early-Years-Foundation-Stage-EYM.pdf (accessed 16 August 2021).

Department for Education (DfE) (2014) *The National Curriculum in England: Framework for Key Stages 1–4.* London: HMSO. [online] Available at: https://www.gov.uk/government/publications/national-curriculum-in-england -framework-for-key-stages-1-to-4 (accessed 16 August 2021).

Department for Education (DfE) (2017) *Statutory Framework for Early Years Foundation Stage.* London: HMSO. [online] Available at: https://www.gov.uk/government/uploads/system/uploads/attachment_data/file/596629/EYFS _STATUTORY_FRAMEWORK_2017.pdf (accessed 16 August 2021).

Department for Education (DfE) (2021) *Statutory Framework for Early Years Foundation Stage.* London: HMSO. [online] Available at: https://assets.publishing.service.gov.uk/government/uploads/system/uploads/attachment_data/ file/974907/EYFS_framework_-_March_2021.pdf (accessed 16 August 2021).

Department for Education (DfE) (2021a) *Model Music Curriculum: Key Stage 1 to 3. Non-statutory Guidance for the National Curriculum in England.* London: HMSO. Available at: https://assets.publishing.service.gov.uk /government/uploads/system/uploads/attachment_data/file/974366/Model_Music_Curriculum_Full.pdf (accessed 16 August 2021).

Dewey, J (1938) *Experience and Education.* New York: Touchstone (first Touchstone edition published 1997).

Dweck, C (2006) *Mindset: The New Psychology of Success.* New York: Ballantine Books.

Eisner, E (2002) *The Arts and the Creation of Mind.* New Haven and London: Yale University Press.

Elders, L (2017) *Schools without Walls: Case Studies.* Funded by the Paul Hamlyn Foundation (unpublished).

Ericsson, K A (2016) *Peak: Secrets from the New Science of Expertise.* New York: Houghton Mifflin Harcourt.

Fawcett, M and Hay, P (2004) 5x5x5=Creativity in the Early Years. *International Journal of Art and Design Education,* 23 (3): 234–45. Corsham: NSEAD. Available at: https://onlinelibrary.wiley.com/doi/abs/10.1111/j.1476-8070 .2004.00403.x (accessed 20 August 2021).

Hosack Janes, K (2021) Objects of Curiosity: How Old Master Paintings Have Been Used in the Primary Classroom to Provide Pupils with Cognitive Challenge and Creative Agency. *Thinking Skills and Creativity,* 41.

Lucas, B (2020) *Schools as Testbeds for our Vital Creativity.* Chartered College of Teaching: The Education Exchange. [online] Available at: https://theeducation.exchange/schools-as-testbeds-for-our-vital-creativity/ (accessed 20 August 2021).

Lucas, B and Spencer, E (2017) *Teaching Creative Thinking: Developing Learners Who Generate Ideas and Can Think Critically.* Williston: Crown House Publishing.

Malaguzzi, L (1998) History, Ideas and Basic Philosophy, in Edwards, C P, Gandini, L and Forman, G (eds) *The Hundred Languages of Children: The Reggio Emilia Approach - Advanced Reflections* (second edition). Stamford: Albex, pp 49–97.

Malaguzzi, L. A Hundred Languages (trans. Gandini, L). [online] Available at: https://www.reggiochildren.it/en/reggio -emilia-approach/100-linguaggi-en/ (accessed 2 September 2021).

Marr, A (2013) *A Short Book about Drawing.* London: Quadrille Publishing Ltd.

National Advisory Committee on Creativity and Cultural Education (NACCCE) (1999) All Our Futures: Creativity, Culture and Education. [online] Available at: http://sirkenrobinson.com/pdf/allourfutures.pdf (accessed 28 October 2021).

Office of Standards in Education (Ofsted) (2021) School Inspection Handbook. [online] Available at: https://www.gov .uk/government/publications/school-inspection-handbook-eif/school-inspection-handbook (accessed 16 August 2021).

Organisation for Economic Co-operation and Development (OECD) (2020) PISA in Focus: Do Students Learn in Co-operative or Competitive Environments. OECD. Available at: https://www.oecd-ilibrary.org/education/do -students-learn-in-co-operative-or-competitive-environments_e7a5f3e4-en (accessed 16 August 2021).

Organisation for Economic Co-operation and Development (OECD) (2021) PISA 2022 Creative Thinking. OECD. [online] Available at: https://www.oecd.org/pisa/innovation/creative-thinking/ (accessed 21 August 2021).

Runco, M A and Acar, S (2012) Divergent Thinking as an Indicator of Creative Potential. *Creativity Research Journal*, 24 (1): 66–75.

Schleicher, A (2020) How Can We Foster Creativity in School: And How We Will Know, Conference Keynote Given at 'Codex - Leonardo at 500: Boosting Creativity in Education', Paris. [online] Available at: https://youtu.be/OOvhOV _vUpQ (accessed 23 August 2021).

Shulman, L (2005) Signature Pedagogies in the Professions. *Daedalus*, 134 (3): 52–59.

Thornton, L and Brunton, P (2009) *Understanding the Reggio Approach: Early Years Education in Practice*. London: Routledge.

Torrance, E P (1966) *Torrance Tests of Creative Thinking: Norms-Technical Manual* (research edition). Princeton: Personnel Press.

Watkins, C (2005) *Classrooms as Learning Communities: What's in it for Schools?* Abingdon: Routledge.

Conclusion to Part 2

In this section of the book we have looked at a variety of theoretical and educational frameworks which can aid our understanding of what conditions are most likely to be conducive to nurturing creative development. Some of these may have resonated with you more than others, and hopefully you have enjoyed exploring the subject of creativity from multiple perspectives, finding your own thoughts supported or, just as usefully, challenged.

The following two chapters examine creativity in action through brief case studies of practice that nurture creativity in settings in and beyond schools. Beforehand though, I would like to share with you my own advice that I give to teachers and teacher training students about how they might focus on creating a creative learning environment for children and young people. I find that the following exercise works well as an initial review.

First, (as Dewey recommends) it is important to stop, look and listen. In other words, try observing what is naturally taking place in front of you between learners before adding any new intervention. You will need a stimulus for learning as an impulse (again, to echo Dewey). I would suggest a work of art – from a book or website, or better still the real thing. Alternatively, a stimulus might be, for example, an antique clock, a piece of clothing, a patch of meadow, or an open-ended question written on the board with a relevant image beside it (notice all these examples contain a visual stimulus to encourage curiosity at a glance). A good barometer for knowing if something is a rich enough stimulus is if you find yourself pondering it for a while.

Now watch what happens. Are the pupils keen to ask questions about the stimulus, or do you think they need some gentle guidance? Be careful not to jump in too soon as they will need time to think, especially those children who are comfortable with contemplating things for a while (remember Claxton's notion of the tortoise mind).

Then, think about what strategies might help the learners make their thoughts concrete. It might not be the same for everyone. Some might prefer jotting their thoughts down on rough paper. Others may like to share their thoughts out loud with a partner or into a digital recording device. A combination of these methods might work well. But whichever is chosen, the emphasis should be on experimental thinking instead of asking for finished, polished ideas. Sometimes, if a group of students are writing their ideas down together on a large piece of paper, I ask each of them to use a different colour felt-tip pen so that different voices are made explicit. It is good to see and value lots of points of view.

When the time is right, nudge the thinking along a little by asking 'what if?' type of questions (as Craft recommends) all the while continuing to observe the dynamics of the learning taking place. This whole process need not take longer than 20 minutes, but it will offer plenty of evidence to inform which interventions for nurturing creativity further will be most effective.

When analysing the outcomes from your observations, think about the quality of the learners' engagement with the stimulus and with each other.

- What did you see pupils doing? Were the questions they generated interesting?
- Did they surprise you?
- What did they reveal about the learners?
- Were the questions related to past learning experiences in school, or pupils' lives outside of school?

Also think about how you might describe the outcomes.

- Are there words or phrases you have encountered in this book helpful?
- How do outcomes relate to the theoretical and educational frameworks in Part 2?
- What outcomes would you like to see more of in future sessions, and how might you plan for these?
- Are the three conditions we have been exploring in this book for nurturing creativity helpful for your planning purposes?

The exercise above should enable you to tailor a creative learning environment to the children and young people you want to encourage to be creative. It will focus your mind on the processes that naturally occur, and hopefully lead to you planning process-driven learning opportunities. When planning, as well as thinking about the three conditions for nurturing creativity, you might also what to think about whether you are using the following two 'experiential strategies' (Hosack Janes, 2021, p 10) (Figure 4.1); so called because they reflect Dewey's experiential continuum framework opportunities for pupils: to share and use their prior experiences in order to widen subsequent experiences; to actively participate in the 'development of what is taught' (1938, p 19); and to take part in reciprocal 'co-operative enterprise' (p 72). In my research these experiential strategies can be identified as being present in all process-driven activities and seen to provide pupils with cognitive challenge and creative agency. This is explained in some detail in the next chapter where I look at the National Gallery's Take One Picture scheme.

	Yes, In what ways?	No
Encouraging Individual Responses		
Making Connections		

Figure 4.1 *Experiential strategies planning tool.*

The experiential strategies planning tool below essentially prompts you to establish if the activities you are planning (i) encourage individual responses from pupils, and (ii) make connections between the stimulus for learning and pupils' prior learning (which could be experiences in or out of school). The 'in what ways' area asks you to pinpoint exactly how your planning facilitates these. It is important when thinking about encouraging individual responses that the activity moves pupils beyond the parameters of simply practising a technique that has been demonstrated. What you want to include are chances for pupils to personally input something of themselves into their work. In the 'in what ways' area you might write, for example, through 'pair talk', 'group discussion', 'role play', or 'experimenting with materials', or 'working towards a final piece that is not predetermined', adding more detail if you find it useful. In other words, the planning tool helps you to avoid planning activities where impulses are seen as purposes (see Chapter 3).

Part 3

Creative conditions in action

5 Creative conditions in schools: examples of practice

The testing of ideas in a variety of contexts is known as 'practical theorising', meaning 'looking for attractive ideas for practice and subjecting these ideas to critical examination' (Hagger and McIntyre, 2006, p 58). We shall be using such an approach in this chapter as we examine the following case studies that concentrate on developing pupils' creativity in the classroom. As you read the following examples of practice, you should take time to critically examine each one in relation to your own experiences of teaching and learning. Try to notice if the pedagogical approaches also resonate with what you have read in the theoretical and educational frameworks in Part 2 of this book. In particular, try and reflect on the differences between social and institutional contexts in each case study, and think about your own priorities for learners. In addition, see if the conditions for nurturing creativity put forward so far in this book apply to each example of practice. This is a way of analysing whether learners in the case studies have been offered similar opportunities to the ones that were shown to be common in the experiences of people well-known for being creative, explored in Part 1. Namely, think about the extent each case study encourages valuing the arts in everyday life, promotes experimentation and play, and provides opportunities to collaborate with others.

By investigating pedagogical practice from a number of perspectives – that of others with your own – the process is a collective, co-constructed endeavour. Such an approach regards the learner (teacher as learner in this case) as central to the formation of purpose, as advocated by Dewey (1938) (discussed in Chapter 3). Such a stance views teacher education as a 'multidisciplinary and collaborative field of inquiry, and a source of knowledge generation that fulfils a pressing and fundamental need in society', as defined in the positional paper on the Intellectual Basis of Teacher Education (UCET, 2020) from the Universities' Council for the Education of Teachers.

Unapologetically, the examples of practice that we will look at in this chapter include a focus on the arts. There are good reasons for this. First, because valuing the arts in everyday life is one of the conditions identified in this book as important for nurturing creativity. Second, because the arts are a fertile central stimulus for teaching and learning across curriculum subject areas. With this in mind, I will start by describing a scheme that is very close to my heart because I managed it while I was head of schools at the National Gallery, London. It is a scheme for primary schools called Take One Picture. You may remember from Chapter 3 I discussed findings from my own research based on it.

The National Gallery's Take One Picture scheme

This long-running scheme encourages primary school teachers to use a single painting from the UK's nationally owned collection of Western European paintings (dating between the 13th and 19th centuries, housed at the National Gallery) for teaching and learning across the curriculum. The Gallery has a statutory responsibility to make the collection accessible to the public, with its foremost aim '*to establish a central role for Old Master paintings in modern cultural life*' (The National Gallery, 2017, p 2). Therefore, as part of a number of initiatives organised by the Gallery to fulfil this remit, the Take One Picture scheme has been offered annually to UK primary schools since 1995. The scheme has no rules as to how teachers make use of a painting in the classroom, and therefore how a project is undertaken is decided at school level.

The Take One Picture scheme started after head teacher, Mark Hazzard, visited the Gallery shop and returned to school with a resource pack on the subject of the *Wilton Diptych* (c. 1395–9), a fourteenth-century devotional altarpiece created by an unknown artist. The teaching resource comprised a printed reproduction of the original painting and some notes on its content and history. Over the period of a school term, pupils at the teacher's school studied the painting, including learning how it was made. Covering curriculum subject areas such as history, English, science, design technology and religious education, as well as art and design, pupils learnt about the life of Richard II (depicted in the painting), King of England from 1377 to 1399; they investigated the stories of the saints shown standing next to him; they found out about heraldry; experimented with making their own primary colour pigments; mixed egg tempera (the paint used in the diptych produced from pigment and egg yolk); and among many other activities, practised the art of gilding. When the project was finished the teacher contacted the Gallery's Education Department. This resulted in the pupils' work being mounted in a display in the Gallery's Education Centre in 1994.

Every year, since 1995 to the present day, based on the same idea of one painting being used as a central stimulus for teaching and learning across the curriculum, the Gallery challenges UK primary schools to respond to a selected painting from the collection.

The Gallery runs a (chargeable) one-day teachers' course as part of the scheme. This focuses on the selected painting for that year, giving teachers the opportunity to see the original painting in the Gallery (unless delegates are online) and to find out about it from Gallery curators. During the course, teachers are also shown examples of how schools have responded to previous Take One Picture paintings.

Printed reproductions (in poster form) of current and previous Take One Picture paintings are available to purchase from the Gallery shop. On the Gallery website downloadable digital images and teachers' notes for each Take One Picture painting are accessible free of charge. The teachers' notes give basic information about the content and context of a painting; a small amount of biographical information about the artist; and some suggestions for introducing the painting to a class and possible curriculum links.

Teachers are encouraged to send photographs and brief descriptions to the Gallery demonstrating how their class, or school, have responded to the selected painting for that year, with the view to the Gallery mounting an annual Take One Picture exhibition each summer (in the Gallery and online). Attending the teachers' course is not a requirement for submitting work for consideration.

In my former role as head of schools at the National Gallery, I curated four Take One Picture exhibitions between 2004 and 2007. Curating the exhibitions involved visiting schools from across the UK to choose work to display. Decisions were based on representing a variety of responses and taking into account how well exhibits might work together in an exhibition space. During these school visits teachers discussed with me how positively they believed using a painting as a central stimulus had affected their own teaching and pupils' learning. These discussions led to me undertaking research (Hosack Janes, 2021) into the nature of the pedagogies employed by teachers using a painting in this way.

On analysis, data from the research – involving 25 teachers from five schools – revealed that there were two distinct ways that teachers used an old master painting as a central stimulus for teaching and learning. The first way was to inspire art making. The second was as an object (a source) of curiosity, where pupils were encouraged to make links between their own experiences and the content of the painting, and where teachers assisted pupils in making connections between the painting and other stimuli.

Those teachers who saw the Take One Picture scheme primarily as learning about and enjoying art tended to plan art-making activities (the first way). In contrast, those teachers who had a broader curriculum understanding of the scheme planned substantially more activities that used the painting as a hook for learning across subject areas (the second way). Although there is no reason why the first and second approach should be mutually exclusive, it was found that teachers who used a painting to solely inspire art making mainly planned activities that were technique- and product-driven. These activities had premeditated end goals for which step-by-step instructions were given to pupils. Pupil outcomes from these activities tended to be very similar to each other. In most instances it was difficult to tell pupils' work apart, or to see differences from what the teacher (or artistic practitioner in some cases) had demonstrated.

Conversely, it was found that the teachers who used a painting as an object of curiosity employed strategies which can be described as experiential in nature. This is because the activities followed closely Dewey's (1938) *'impulse'* (p 67), *'plan'* (p 71), *'end-view'* (p 67) model of learning (as described in Chapter 3). The pedagogy was shown to be ideas- and process-driven, involving teachers and pupils cooperating in the formation of purposes. An example of this includes one teacher who wrote in her log journal (a method of data collection used in the study) how she discussed with her class the 'rough outline' of a project that focused on the Early Italian Renaissance painting *Saint George and the Dragon* (c. 1470) by Paolo Uccello. She explained how she 'adapted ... plans accordingly' based on the pupils' initial responses to the painting. She wrote that the pupils 'were very keen to include drama, but found it difficult to suggest what this could entail, apart from a fight scene! So, she assisted them in turning the idea into an educationally purposeful 'end-view' (Dewey, 1938, p 67) by showing them how to create a living frieze.

Such a reciprocal teacher–pupil 'co-operative enterprise' (p 71), or exchange, was revealed in all of the planned activities by teachers who employed the second object of curiosity approach. This was identified as two experiential strategies: (i) encouraging individual responses beyond the parameters of practising an art technique; and (ii) making connections between the painting and other stimuli and/or with pupils' known previous experiences. In another example where reciprocal teacher–pupil co-operative exchange could be identified, a teacher wanted to encourage pupils to 'express opinions' about how 'we can work alongside the natural world' after looking together at the seventeenth-century Dutch painting *A View of Het Steen in the Early Morning* (probably 1636) by Peter Paul Rubens. The teacher wrote extensively in her log journal about how the project evolved out of the pupils being 'very curious about the blurry image of the windmill in the background of the painting'. She noted the following pupil outcomes from a visit to a windmill that she planned in response to their enquiries:

> At the windmill the children were able to explore all parts of the building and the machinery. They sketched the building from the outside ... asked questions about the sails ... The miller explained the process of grinding wheat into flour, showed the children how the enormous wheels ground the grains and let them feel different sorts of flour. They ended the visit by choosing flours to take back to school to use to bake bread.

> All the children became immersed in this series of activities. They were inspired and focused by the windmill in the painting and thrilled to see it come to life. Their detailed writing and enthusiasm for other related activities was clear and they talked about the windmill using very specific language. ... I think the level of interest comes not only from the visit itself, but also from that initial curiosity aroused by the painted image.

A further example of teacher–pupil co-operative exchange was from an Early Years Foundation Stage teacher who planned a whole class discussion with 4–5 year-olds looking at *The Fighting Temeraire* (1839) by the English painter J.M.W Turner. She asked the children what they noticed in the picture, writing on the whiteboard what they saw. They noticed a ship (the subject of the painting), water, clouds and the sun. The children interpreted the horizon as a wall, giving the teacher the opportunity to introduce new terminology. A flag was spotted on top of a mast, and sails. The ship was thought to be sailing away from an island, and thus used as a starting point for an extended writing task additionally stimulated by the teacher hiding a message in a bottle for the children to find. The teacher read aloud how a boy called Will was stranded on the island and needed their help. The pupils wrote letters back to him, and also made pictures showing what they might be able to see through a telescope if they stood on the deck of the ship (some examples are shown in Figure 5.1).

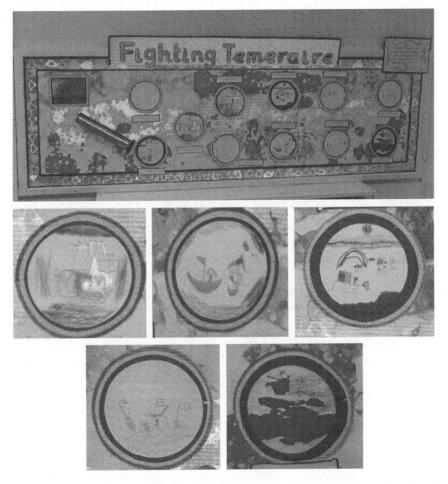

Figure 5.1 *'Telescope' pictures of the imagined view from the deck of the Fighting Temeraire, created by 4–5 year-old pupils.*

Relationships between teachers and their pupils in these three examples of co-operative exchange within the *'plan'* stage (Dewey, 1938, p 71) are shown to be balanced. There is clear intent from the teachers to encourage pupils to make individual responses, and to advance pupils' learning by building on their prior experiences, deliberately helping them to make further connections. For this to happen the pupils need to be involved in the development of the learning. This process is not incidental. It is planned for. It is a process that allows pupils time to think and to share their ideas, providing conditions for nurturing creativity concentrated on in this book. The teacher–pupil relationship also embodies Dewey's belief that a worthwhile educational environment is one where '*the adult can exercise the wisdom his own wider experience gives him without imposing a merely external control*' (Dewey, 1938, p 38).

Moreover, the opportunity for pupils and their teachers to collaborate with others beyond their school is facilitated by the Take One Picture scheme with the chance for pupils' work to be exhibited in the Gallery and on its website. As described in Chapter 3, such a possibility enables one inspiration to inspire others in a '*cycle of creativity*' (Hosack Janes, 2014, p 100) that can connect people across time, place and cultures. And indeed, it was one head teacher's vision for using one painting for teaching and learning across many subject areas that kick-started the whole scheme.

Artful Thinking (Project Zero)

Likewise, with the core premise that '*works of art are good things to think about*' (Tishman and Palmer, 2006, p 5) Harvard University's Graduate School, as part of their ongoing Project Zero research into arts education, have developed a programme called Artful Thinking '*to help teachers regularly use works of visual art and music in their curriculum in ways that strengthen student thinking and learning*' (p 4). This is achieved through a series of '*thinking routines*' (p 9) that are intended to develop '*thinking dispositions*' that include '*questioning and investigating, observing and describing, reasoning, exploring viewpoints, comparing and connecting, and finding complexity*' (p 8). We are told in the final report of a research project that accompanied the development of the programme that these dispositions were chosen for two reasons. First, because each '*represents forms of thinking that are powerful in terms of exploring and appreciating works of art*'. Second, because each '*represents forms of thinking that are powerful in terms of building understanding in other disciplines*' (p 9).

Key to how the thinking routines are used in schools – which are described as '*short, easy-to-learn procedure that help students enact thinking-dispositional behavior*' (p 9) – is pupils become well practiced in applying them to different stimuli and learning contexts. Such an approach is comparable to how Claxton (2021) (see Chapter 3) views '*dispositions*' (which he also calls habits of mind, attributes and mindsets), where he believes an emphasis on teaching approaches that develop these '*over time*' helps them '*grow in strength, complexity and breadth of application*' (p78). Lucas and Spencer's (2017) list of '*habits*' and '*sub-habits*' (p 23) (see Chapter 4), which include, for example, '*using intuition, making connections, playing with possibilities*' (p 22), are also comparable to dispositions that are expected to be honed over time with '*methods which are most likely to lead to the desired capability*' (p 7).

A simple example of a thinking routine is '*I See/I Think/I Wonder*'. It is an activity that is designed '*for exploring works of art and other interesting things*' (p 26) and aims to develop questioning and investigating skills by '*emphasizing asking questions as a way of stimulating curiosity and guiding inquiry'* (p 25). It works as follows, as described on the Project Zero website:

> *Ask students to make an observation about an object—it could be an artwork, image, artifact, or topic—and follow up with what they think might be going on or what they think this observation might be. Encourage students to back up their interpretation with reasons. Ask students to think about what this makes them wonder about the object or topic.*

> *The routine works best when a student responds by using the three stems together at the same time, i.e., 'I see …, I think …, I wonder …'. However, you may find that students begin using one stem at a time, and that you need to scaffold each response with a follow-up question for the next stem.*

> *The routine works well in a group discussion but in some cases you may want to ask students to try the routine individually on paper or in their heads before sharing out as a class. Student responses to the routine can be written down and recorded so that a class chart of observations, interpretations, and wonderings are listed for all to see and returned to during the course of study.*

I have used this routine many times with pupils and teachers taking a painting as a stimulus. I particularly like the way that each question increases in sophistication/ cognitive demand. The 'I see' or 'What can I see?' prompts the listing of items – I can see a clock, the sky, a boy playing football, a house. Then, 'I think' or 'What do I think about what I see?' encourages a higher level of thinking – I think the clock tells what time of the day the people in the painting are leaving to go home from work. Finally, 'I wonder' asks the viewer to think beyond what they can see in the painting – I wonder what period of history the people in the painting belong to, and what the inside of the house might look like, and what the people might be having for their evening meal.

Another thinking routine, this time aiming to develop the disposition of exploring viewpoints, is called the *'Circle of Viewpoints'* routine. The idea is that it helps pupils to see and explore multiple perspectives by trying to understand *'that different people can have different kinds of connections to the same thing, and that these different connections influence what people see and think'*. On the Project Zero website it is presented as follows.

1. *Brainstorm a list of different perspectives.*

2. *Choose one perspective to explore, using these sentence-starters:*

- *I am thinking of … [the topic] … from the viewpoint of … [the viewpoint you've chosen]*

- *I think … [describe the topic from your viewpoint. Be an actor—take on the character of your viewpoint]*

- *A question I have from this viewpoint is … [ask a question from this viewpoint]*

Other thinking routines include, for example: 'Claim/Support/Question', 'Think/Pair/ Share', 'Perceive/Know/Care about', 'Think/Puzzle/Explore', 'Beginning/Middle/End' and 'I used to think/Now I think'.

The research that informed the design of the thinking routines used qualitative methodologies that tried to assess the value of them for pupils (you may remember our discussions in Chapter 4 about difficulties with measuring impact). The researchers (Tishman and Palmer, 2006) argue that the Artful Thinking project could not have been effectively evaluated by 'high-stakes standardised tests' because these 'often foreground low-end cognition' (p 61). Instead, each thinking routine was assessed from the perspectives of the students and their teachers for aspects such as levels of engagement. These evaluations were used to develop thinking routines further so they could be offered as a free resource for teachers. Even though the initial development of the routines was for 14–15 year-olds, the developers hope that they are useful for all school-aged pupils. The study was also able to report that over a two-year period students were noticeably internalising some of the routines.

The Embodying Mathematics Project

Ten schools participated in the Embodying Mathematics Project with Sheffield Hallam University Institute of Education and the theatre company Complicité (who we heard in Chapter 1 works closely with Marcus du Sautoy in his position as the Simonyi Professor for the Public Understanding of Science and Professor of Mathematics at the University of Oxford). The aim of the project was to develop resources for primary school teachers that focus on 'drama informed mathematical movement activities' (Boylan and Reaney, 2018, p 7). The idea came about because Complicité had been exploring with school groups a range of activities they had developed with actors during the creative process of devising the play A Disappearing Number – which tells the true story of a collaboration between Srinivasa Ramanujan and G H Hardy. Here are two examples of these activities as they are presented on the Complicité website.

Partition theory
One of the mathematical formulae that Ramanujan and Hardy worked on together predicted the amount of partitions that a number has. The partition number is the number of ways that an integer can be expressed as a sum.

For example, there are three partitions of 3:   *1+1+1*

2+1 and

3

There are five partitions of 4:   *1+1+1+1*

2+1+1

2+2

3+1 and

4

As the number gets even slightly bigger the number of possible partitions quickly becomes very large.

In groups of five, six or seven arrange yourselves spatially into all the possible configurations for your group number. Pay particular attention to the order you choose to do the partitions in and how you move between the various arrangements.

How do you remember the moves?

Does the number of people in your group lead to a particular set of shapes, spaces and movements?

Does the final sequence of movements suggest a dramatic narrative or dance?

Another exercise that schools took part in is called *Layering stories*:

Choose three sources that have only oblique connections: perhaps a newspaper story, a photo and a poem. In groups find a way to integrate or layer all three sources and find one moment where the three sources come together or converge in some way.

This is a very open-ended task which is often used in our devising process, demanding a high level of inventiveness and experimentation. The results are unpredictable and generally chaotic but from these improvisions we can start to see what is alive and resonant.

The process of devising involves experimenting and discarding numerous ideas, throwing ideas together and allowing the possibility of the unexpected. Simon McBurney [director of A Disappearing Number] frequently describes this process as chaotic but the exploration throws up often collective 'ah ha' moments of revelation. Mathematics works in the same exploratory way.

(Alexander et al, 2007; with permission from Complicité)

The Embodying Mathematics Project has developed this education work further. Professional development workshops and lesson activities were led and evaluated by a team including Victoria Gould, the artistic collaborator who co-wrote the Complicité activities (above), and lecturers from Sheffield Hallam University.

As was acknowledged by the Artful Thinking programme researchers, the Embodying Mathematics Project report recognises that an evaluation of the impact of the project through test results is unreliable in assessing the potential value of such an initiative. Instead, qualitative data from surveys, interviews and feedback from workshop days is claimed to give a fuller picture of the features teachers most appreciated.

Some key outcomes for teachers include 'changes in beliefs about mathematical ability', positive feelings towards 'the capacity to develop a learning community in the classroom', and 'experiences of teacher agency in developing and adapting activities' (Boylan and Reaney, 2018, p 11). The last two points highlight how mathematics teaching lends itself to an experiential model of learning, where mathematics as a subject is viewed as something to be interpreted, and therefore experimented with. Quotes incorporated into Complicité's teachers' notes on their website reiterate the same message, stating *'Mathematics is not a spectator sport – George M Phillips'* and *'A mathematician is a pattern searcher. Maths is about finding patterns in the chaos of numbers that surround us – Marcus du Sautoy'*.

The Embodying Mathematics Project evaluation also reports how teachers perceived the activities had *'a positive influence on pupil attitudes to learning'* and that activities had *'developed a sense of togetherness in the class'* (p 12). However, one barrier to implementing the activities was pressure on curriculum time to complete sessions. This was also an issue for the project described in the next case study.

Bath Children's Literature Festival

We have already seen in this chapter how the scheme Take One Picture focuses on a painting being used in the primary classroom as a central stimulus for cross-curricular teaching and learning. This case study looks at how a deputy head teacher, Jane Howie-Lee (who was also the English subject lead at her primary school), used a book as a stimulus for learning across a number of subject areas with her class. Alongside Jane, I evaluated this work as part of a pilot project for Bath Children's Literature Festival.

The aims of the pilot research project were three-fold. First, to explore the potential a book has for being used as a central stimulus for teaching and learning across curriculum subjects. Second, to explore if the qualitative research methods adopted for the pilot project proved useful as reflective tools. Finally, to explore ways in which a school partnership with Bath Children's Literature Festival might work.

Data collection methods included interviews that took place during site visits to the school in the form of *'professional conversations'* (Kvale, 2007, p 5) between the head teacher (Louise Crocker), Jane and myself. Also, the compilation of a log journal by Jane contained written teacher objectives, activity planning and evidence of pupil outcomes.

The teacher's objectives for the project were (in her own words):

- *to enhance the wider learning experiences of the children by taking a creative approach to exploring a text;*

- *to accelerate progress and improve attainment, by providing challenge and opportunities for children to explore their own interests within the wider historical context of the text;*

- *to use a variety of approaches to exploring the text through art, personal research, DT, writing, visitors, music, science, Children's University, drama, dance.*

The focus book, chosen by the school because it marked the centenary of votes for (most) women in the UK, was *Fantastically Great Women Who Changed the World* by Kate Pankhurst. It is illustrated in full colour by the author who is a descendant of Emmeline

Pankhurst, one of the women featured. The author was one of the guests that year at the literature festival, so one of the advantages of the school partnership was to have a trip arranged for the pupils to meet her in person.

The findings of the evaluation were aligned to the teacher-generated objectives (above), divided into five categories, some of which overlapped. They were as follows.

Category 1: enhancing the wider learning experiences of children

The word 'enhancing' describes the teacher's aim to extend pupils' wider prior learning experiences. There was evidence that this aim was met during the project. Examples in the planning demonstrate that pupils' prior knowledge was sought in relation to the stimulus book, including how the teacher introduced the book to the pupils. She encouraged them to share and read pages together and to talk about the ones that particularly interested them. The strategy is experiential because it ensures learning falls *'within the scope of ordinary life experiences'* (Dewey, 1938, p 73). On a practical level, the activity was possible because the school was given two copies of the book from Bath Festivals and purchased a further three copies themselves. The teachers' log journal comments record (an example quote is given below) how by encouraging individual responses this enabled pupils to share what they already knew:

> One pupil interjected about the author, saying 'I know! Her grandmother was Emmeline Pankhurst. She got votes for women! We named our baby after her'.

The teacher also notes that:

> The girls in the group were particularly horrified to hear that women had not been able to vote.

This led to a wider discussion on democracy. The teacher also wrote about how another pupil made the link between her own arm, which had recently been broken, and Marie Curie and the pictures of X-rays in the book.

During my visit to the school, I noted how readily pupils made references to their own experiences, linking them with the famous women in the book.

Category 2: taking a creative approach to exploring the text

It is apparent from the teacher's planning in the log journal that activities are very process-driven, meaning that the teacher had very clear ideas about which skills she wanted pupils to develop, yet, the actual pupil outcomes were not premeditated (therefore not product-driven). This is an experiential pedagogical approach because it allows pupils to input into the development of what is being taught. It could also be viewed as a creative approach to teaching and learning because pupils are given the opportunity to input as individuals, and therefore able to show their own originality. An example of such planning includes pupils reviewing their trip to Bath Children's Literature Festival where they attended a workshop by the author. The teacher writes:

> *This revisiting activity is very much pupil led ... I want pupils to be able to recall their trip and the presentation given by Kate Pankhurst. I want children to discuss the author's skills and the necessary attributes an author needs ... Finally, I want the children to start to think about how we could apply Kate's ideas in a new way.*

The outcomes of this activity are recorded by the teacher as follows:

> *The group were very keen to share their feelings about Kate's presentation and her ideas. They also found the Guildhall itself fascinating and commented on the ornate ceiling and rich paintings. Several children talked about choosing to sketch the chandeliers. Initially the children were unsure about how we could apply Kate's ideas in a new way, but once one child set the ball rolling with 'Inventions that Changed the World' this generated lots more ideas.*

These ideas were used by the pupils to create their own books based on the idea *Fantastically Great ...*

Category 3: accelerating progress and improving attainment by providing challenge

From the photographs of pupils' work and teacher comments contained in the log journal based on conversations with pupils, it is evident that the opportunity for pupils to write their own book was a challenge relished. The teacher writes:

> *One child, who had seemed to lack engagement, suddenly came alive at the idea of writing a book about Great Artists who Changed the World. She went to the school library to search for information about artists.*

Other titles of pupils' books include *The Most Dangerous Disasters of All Time* and *Men Who Changed the World*. Unfortunately, due to time restrictions these books were not finished before the end of the academic year.

Category 4: accelerating progress and improving attainment by giving opportunities for children to explore their own interests within the context of the text

Examples given so far show that there is evidence to suggest that the teacher's objective to give pupils the opportunity to explore their own interests within the context of the text was fulfilled. Another example of this includes pupils producing individual self-portraits after studying together the self-portraits of Frida Kahlo (another woman who featured in the stimulus book). The teacher writes movingly about how one of the pupils engaged with this activity:

> *One boy was able to articulate the message he was trying to achieve in his portrait. He found his voice and impressed his peers with his ideas. He was able to manage impulsive behaviour and maintained focus for a long period of time. He was visibly blossoming.*

Pupils also explored their own interests within the context of the text by jointly writing to the author, posing questions that they collectively decided they wanted to find out about the book. Some of these questions are presented below.

- Why did you choose to write about women?

- Why did you choose these particular women?

- How long did it take you to create the book?

- How long did it take you to illustrate the book, and was it done by hand or using computer technology?

- Was this book your initial idea or did it change?

- Are you writing a new book? If so, what is it about?

The teacher remarked on how thrilled the pupils were to receive a reply from the author with all their questions answered.

Category 5: using a variety of approaches to explore the text through art, personal research, DT, writing, visitors, music, science, Children's University, drama, dance

Overall, the project did involve pupils creating works of art. This was in the form of self-portraits (as described) and illustrating their book covers. Pupils undertook personal research into the famous women in the stimulus book (in many cases unprompted by the teacher) and they researched subjects in order to write their own books. Although a visitor did not come to the school, instead the pupils attended the author's workshop at Bath Children's Literature Festival and remembered not only aspects of the author's presentation, but also the impressive venue of the Guildhall. In addition, pupils had the advantage of meeting the author after her talk and receiving a letter from her answering their questions. There was, however, no music, science, Children's University, drama or dance activities planned for by the teacher.

The evaluation concluded that the teacher's three objectives for using a book as a central stimulus for teaching and learning across curriculum subject areas had been met, although in places only to some extent due to time pressures curtailing some potential learning. This included the pupils not being able to finish writing their own books in school, and there was not enough time to explore possible outcomes in all of the curriculum subject areas anticipated. This point could be addressed in future school projects with either an increase in time allocated to a project in a school, or less ambitious initial objectives.

It was notable that the nature of teaching and learning during the project was experiential, meaning that the teacher designed activities so that pupils were able to use their prior experiences to inform and extend their learning. Activities were designed to involve pupils in discussions and decision-making, and these informed the development of the project. It is also notable that the visit to the author's workshop at the Bath Children's Literature

Festival was a memorable experience for the pupils and one which was consolidated by the teacher's decision to reflect on what the pupils remembered and to use points drawn out from discussions to shape further pupil learning experiences.

The data in the log journal compiled by the teacher proved extremely useful for analysing the project against the teacher-generated objectives and the main aims of the pilot research project. It revealed in detail why and how the project was operationalised at a school level. My visits to the school were important too for building good professional relationships with the teacher and head teacher and for gathering background information to contextualise the data contained in the teacher's log journal.

Class song

This final case study similarly demonstrates how one teacher uses an arts stimulus to achieve multiple objectives. This time the focus is a song. Well, several songs in fact, because it is something this teacher embeds into his planning on an annual basis. He started using the idea of a class song in his first year as a newly qualified teacher, and has evolved the process ever since. I interviewed the teacher in question, Mr Looker-Jones, for this book. After our initial 'hellos', I asked him how the idea for a class song – a personalised song that his class collaboratively creates each year – came about. This is précised version of the transcript:

> The rationale behind the 'class song' originally was partly because I wanted to establish myself at the school. Doing something unique and slightly different. To carve out a little niche for myself, which I think it did quite quickly.

> My class was called Beijing [classes were named after Olympic cities], and I'm not quite sure how, but I somehow got the idea that 'I Just Can't Wait to be King' [a song from the Disney classic 'The Lion King'] could be 'I Just Can't Wait for Beijing'. I had Year 3 and 4 [pupils] that first year. So, I had the idea before I went into school that I really wanted to make an impact in the first 'move up' day [the first time he met his class]. This was in the July before I was due to start. I just wanted to win the kids over! It was like marketing myself to the kids really, showing that it was going to be a fun year and I was going to be a fun teacher. And just to connect as a team.

> On the day, we came up with about fifty per cent of the song, which was all about just enjoying school and enjoying the different lessons. There were lines in there about enjoying reading, writing and arithmetic. … And French est formidable! And about school in general really.

I asked him where the backing music came from:

> I searched the karaoke version of the song, and we sang our own lyrics over the top. … And because it was a Disney song they [the pupils] were all familiar with it, so you don't have to teach them the melody … That cuts a massive part of the process out … It makes it easier for them to fit their lyrics to the timing of the song.

That age group [Year 3 and 4] absolutely loved it, and I remember we finished our sharing assembly with it [which happened in the Summer term]. And all the children were running around the edge of the hall, and they held hands at the end of it. So, it kind of physically, as well as through the lyrics, gave the message that we were a team … I think we all felt we were in it together.

Whenever we did music, whenever we did any singing that year, we would sing our song as well … They [the pupils] felt incredibly proud … Other teachers would say to me 'I've heard all about this song'. They [the pupils] were turning it into a news agenda … It gave me a lot of confidence … The class song was the finalé in the sharing assembly, and that became a blueprint for the future.

I asked him to describe the process of getting the pupils to write the lyrics:

It was very different that year because they were younger … Some of them would have still been in Year 2 at that point [all the other class songs have been with Year 5 and 6 pupils]. They [the Year 2 pupils] were sitting in table groups with their friends – there were some groups of 6, there were some 4s – they were coming up with an idea and then I was kind of squeezing that to fit the syllables and beat of the music … It wasn't too difficult. You know [if a pupil said] 'I want to do something about sport', so, you know, we thought about that together, and sang what we had. And at that stage they were new to me, and they were slightly shy about it, I suppose. But once we came back [at the beginning of term in September] they got behind it, and we were good to go.

I asked if it would be true to say, while they were writing the song, if he was able to find out about the pupils, as well as them finding out about him.

Absolutely, yes, definitely. And that's what those move up days are all about – you finding out about them and them finding out about you. Yes, that was very much a big part of it.

He then described how he got from there to doing a class song each year.

I think the success of that – it was such a good activity for the move up day … I wanted the next one to also be meaningful and I also wanted to champion the arts straight away. We talked a lot about that on our PGCE course.

So, I was given Year 5 and 6 … At the time they felt like teenagers to me … I felt a huge sense of responsibility … And even more than in the first year [of teaching] I felt I had to win them [the pupils] over, so choosing the song that year was different. I tried to pick a more contemporary, and kind of trendy song, something that I knew they would get behind. My class was then [called] Rio, and there is a film called Rio, an animation film aimed at a slightly older audience. So, again, I just looked through the sound track – I wasn't familiar with any of those songs – and found one that could work as a class song.

The original lyrics were 'Let me take you to Rio', so we changed it to 'Come and join us in Rio'. And to win them [the pupils] over more, I thought we'd make the song about them individually. So that was the first year that it actually became more about the children. And because they were older I felt I could split the song up into lines. I counted how many kids there were and how many lines, making sure that would all fit. And then I would say, 'right you two, your lines need to rhyme, go and write something about yourself'. … They were amazing … We had such funny lines … And the parents really loved it. … So, yes, it was a huge hit again … And I didn't know those children at all. I hadn't taught them … And so again it was me getting to know them. You got some of them saying they wanted to write about dancing and singing and acting, and then some coming up with other lines that get you to see their personality straight away. It really is a fantastic activity actually for getting to know your class.

… And it's easy to overlook how many skills are being used … They're writing their own lyrics and they're making them fit to the music, and they're performing.

The following year – that was lovely because I then got back the kids I had the first year … I had taught all of those children before. That was really a joyous year for me. I think I could have said anything to them and they would have gone with it. We had another Disney song. One from 'Hercules'. … Called 'Zero to Hero' … We had lots of sporty kids that year, and they were all on board. And it was really light-hearted and funny and we were doing Greece as our theme in the first term, so that all linked together really nicely.

I asked, if he remembers each class by their song.

Yes, very much, and because I make a DVD for the kids, I have a lovely memory of each year … It's a little time capsule that captures that moment …

The year afterwards we did One Direction's 'Best Song Ever'. All we needed to do was swap 'song' for 'class' … so it became 'Best Class Ever'. The fewer lyrics you need to change on the chorus the better … It was really popular because it was of the moment. They all knew that song really well. Quite an anthem, with a really strong message about everyone in it together.

I asked if the message was linked to a PSRE (Personal, Social and Religious Education) activity.

No, not really … [laughing] … it's more of a PR type of thing [laughing]. But it does work! It's to do with mutual respect and trust. We're all in this together is definitely the key.

Another year was Rita Ora's 'Anywhere'. I just absolutely loved that song at the time, and I couldn't find a song. … I was almost worried that it was slightly melancholic. But it just worked. I remember their [the pupils'] reaction when I said what the song was going to be. They said, 'wow'. They were really pleased. The following year it was Taylor Swift, and this year it's Dua Lipa. We're really on trend [he laughs].

In Chapter 4 we talked about how in England the Office for Standards in Education (Ofsted) make a judgement about the quality of education in a school based partly on an assessment by inspectors on '*the extent to which schools are equipping pupils with the knowledge and cultural capital they need to succeed in life*' (Ofsted, 2021, p 204). The case studies in this chapter have covered a range of examples of 'cultural capital', from old master paintings to modern non-fiction books to contemporary pop music. Exposing pupils to as wide a breadth of cultural highlights as possible supports the valuing the arts in everyday life condition for nurturing creativity identified in this book.

REFLECTIVE POINTS

- Have you been involved in any initiatives in a school that have had the prime objective to develop pupils' creativity? If so, how well do you think the objective was met? Did some aspects work more effectively than others?

- Take a look at the latest Take One Picture exhibition on the National Gallery website and critically evaluate examples of children's work in terms of whether you consider pupils' creativity has been developed.

- One of the key outcomes from the Embodying Mathematics Project was that teachers experienced '*agency in developing and adapting activities*' (Boylan and Reaney, 2018, p 11). Consider how you might adapt some of the suggested classroom activities from the teachers' pack for *A Disappearing Number* and the Artful Thinking thinking routines.

- Consider the ways in which the impact of the case studies in this chapter have been presented and think about how you might gather qualitative data yourself that provides useful information about the creative development of pupils that aids reflection.

Further reading

Hosack Janes, K (2014) *Using the Visual Arts for Cross-Curricular Teaching and Learning*. Abingdon: Routledge.

References

Alexander, C, Gould, V and Freedman, N (2007) A Disappearing Number, resources pack for teachers. [online] Available at: http://www.complicite.org/media/1438093193ADN_online_workpack.pdf (accessed 3 June 2021).

Boylan, M and Reaney, S (2018) The Embodying Mathematics Project Report. [online] Available at: https://shura.shu.ac.uk/22326/1/The%20Embodying%20Mathematics%20Project%20Report%20%20%20August%2018.pd (accessed 2 July 2021).

Claxton, G (2021) *The Future of Teaching and the Myths that Hold it Back*. Abingdon: Routledge.

Dewey, J (1938) *Experience and Education*. New York: Touchstone (first Touchstone edition published 1997.

Hagger, H and McIntyre, D (2006) *Learning Teaching from Teachers: Realising the Potential of School-Based Teacher Education*. Maidenhead: Open University Press.

Hosack Janes, K (2014) *Using the Visual Arts for Cross-Curricular Teaching and Learning*. Abingdon: Routledge.

Hosack Janes, K (2021) Objects of Curiosity: How Old Master Paintings Have Been Used in the Primary Classroom to Provide Pupils with Cognitive Challenge and Creative Agency. *Thinking Skills and Creativity*, 41.

Kvale, S (2007) *Doing Interviews*. London: Sage.

Lucas, B and Spencer, E (2017) *Teaching Creative Thinking: Developing Learners Who Generate Ideas and Can Think Critically*. Williston: Crown House Publishing.

Office of Standards in Education (Ofsted) (2021) School Inspection Handbook. [online] Available at: https://www.gov.uk/government/publications/school-inspection-handbook-eif/school-inspection-handbook (accessed 16 August 2021).

Project Zero website. [online] Available at: Harvard Graduate School of Education, http://www.pz.harvard.edu/thinking-routines#CoreThinkingRoutines (accessed 10 September 2021).

The National Gallery (2017) The National Gallery Annual Report and Accounts for the Year Ended 31 March 2017. [online] Available at: https://www.nationalgallery.org.uk/media/24777/annual-report-accounts_2016-17.pdf (accessed 12 March 2021).

The National Gallery Take One Picture website. [online] Available at: https://www.nationalgallery.org.uk/learning/take-one-picture (accessed 1 September 2021).

Tishman, S and Palmer, P (2006) *Artful Thinking: Stronger Thinking and Learning through the Power of Art*. Project Zero, Harvard Graduate School. [online] Available at: http://www.pz.harvard.edu/resources/final-report-artful-thinking (accessed 12 August 2021).

Universities Council for the Education of Teachers (2020) Intellectual Basis of Teacher Education Position Paper. [online] Available at: https://www.ucet.ac.uk/11675/intellectual-base-of-teacher-education-report-updated-february-2020 (accessed 10 September 2021).

6 Creative conditions beyond the classroom: examples of practice

In this final chapter we take a look at whether the three conditions for nurturing creativity that we have been focusing on throughout this book, and which were evident in the examples of school practice in the last chapter, are also present in examples of educational practice that take place in settings other than schools. The intention, as always, is to gain a deeper awareness and understanding of how opportunities can be shaped to support young people (or indeed anyone) in their creative development.

We mainly consider three different projects where drama is central to helping young people to express themselves creatively. First, we find out how the Theatre Royal Bath (where Toby Thompson found an artistic home when he was 13 years old) runs Summer schools, providing young people with the opportunity to develop a play in a week from scratch. Then, we go on to look at how the Mandala Theatre Company, in Oxford, have involved young people affected by knife crime in writing a stage production aimed at raising awareness around associated issues. And then, we examine a project that is putting acting masterclasses online to demonstrate how multiple interpretations of a single classical text can be useful in exploring wider themes.

Create, Play, Perform: summer school at the Theatre Royal Bath Theatre School

In Chapter 1 Toby Thompson described how in his early teens he got involved in a young people's theatre group (YPT Urban) at the Theatre Royal Bath. For him, the experience was life changing. He told me that he viewed this time as '*an initiation*' into an artistic world that he found '*authentic*'. This was due to him being able to work alongside trained theatre makers in a professional theatre. Thankfully, chances for young people to participate in similar high-quality events and classes still exist at the Theatre Royal Bath through their busy education programme.

Based in a specially designed building dedicated to young people's theatre, called the Egg, the Theatre Royal Bath Theatre School runs evening, weekend and school holiday sessions for anybody aged between 5 and 25. The whole character of the place feels supportive in its conception, complete with a womb-like egg-shaped auditorium. There are no auditions for young people to become members, and if the already subsidised costs are a barrier to participating, these can be waived. Membership also means that the young people receive discounts for regularly scheduled live theatre productions.

Alex Duarte-Davies, executive director of the Theatre School, and Sophie Jacobs-Wyburn, the Theatre School artistic director, talked to me about the week-long *Create, Play, Perform* Summer holiday project which sees young people developing a play from scratch together in just five days (even less than a week!).

Collaborating with people of around the same age, the week begins with the group playing a number of physical theatre games where members get to have fun and find out about each other. One of the games is '*Keepie Uppie*', which Sophie uses as an analogy throughout the creating process. '*I say that this game will tell you everything you need to know about theatre making*'. Sophie argues that the game is both about individuals and group dynamics, explaining that the group as a whole is helping each other to achieve the same thing, and that everyone is finding their own way (or ways) of doing it. Some people, Sophie suggests, will be trying to pass the ball in a very controlled way, focusing solely on keeping it in the air. Others will be quite flamboyant in their approach, perhaps doing something balletic, or something risky, like closing their eyes. Each of these ways the group will respond to, may be with delight, or with alarm; both are interesting outcomes. The overall message of the game is that we need a combination of approaches to make the game interesting. Playing it safe will lead to the ball staying in the air (most probably). But taking some risks keeps the game fresh and exciting. Sophie explains that observing how the group supports each other in enabling (or not) to fulfil the common goal of keeping the ball up is fascinating, and this includes what happens when the ball is dropped. How failure is viewed and used within the group is important, as is seeing whether the less flamboyant players attempt more dangerous moves after a while. Links can certainly be made here with Vygotsky's (trans., 1987) sociocultural concept of the zone of proximal development (ZPD) and with other theorists' ideas on the importance of risk-taking and freedom to fail (for example, Claxton (1998) and Craft (2001) – see Chapter 3).

In order to generate material for the play, which Sophie was keen to stress '*genuinely starts from nothing*', members are encouraged to share what music they like listening to. Alex made the point to me that '*everyone is listening to different music these days, so it's a real palette of styles that are shared*'. The young people are asked to talk about other interests too, such as what they like to read, and if they have seen anything at the theatre, cinema or on television they have really enjoyed. All this helps to build a sense of community identity. Alex describes the practice as '*a real plethora of possibilities*'.

The week of collaboration continues with the emergence of three themes, named by Sophie as a '*foundation theme*', a '*visual theme*' and a '*sonic theme*'. These can be blended in endless ways to test ideas for the final performance. In addition, the play comes about by experimenting with teaching methods promoted by the French actor and acting coach Jacques Lecoq. These techniques aim to help the young people discover ways to perform that suit their own creative expression. Looking for personal meaning is key to this process, with the final piece being crafted and recrafted so as to capture the many voices of the ensemble. Again, strong connections can be made here with the sociocultural theorist ideas we examined in Chapter 3, particularly with the work of Dewey (1938, 1934) and Vygotsky (trans., 1978, 2004). Interestingly, although not surprisingly, Simon McBurney, the co-founder of the theatre group Complicité, whose work we have previously looked at in Chapters 1 and 5, trained in the workshops of Jacques Lecoq.

At the mid-week point Sophie asks all members of the group to stop and reflect on what they have achieved so far. This moment tends to feel like there is a need to throw something else into the mix, to get the group to try out some more ideas. '*Not just sticking with something is sometimes what's asked for*', Sophie says, '*even if they end up going back to where they were before*'.

The young people perform their piece on the Egg stage to a live audience of family and friends on the final day. This is a time to celebrate everyone's efforts and enjoy what has been created. I asked Sophie and Alex if genuinely starting from nothing puts the group under a lot of pressure to come up with something of quality in less than a week. They both insist, however, that because members work with quality input from the start – collaborating with professional theatre makers in a working theatre – the environment is conducive to the high expectations, and quality outcomes always transpire. This point is worth paying attention to as it sums up a confidence about a learning culture that thrives on – and indeed needs and expects – experimentation, while at the same time striving to ensure a coherent '*end-view*' (Dewey, 1938, p 67). Alex emphasises that '*the journey to get there is the important thing*'. The process makes the experience worthwhile. It is a safe learning space where creativity is understood to evolve from play, experimentation, shared thoughts and continuous reflection.

During 2020, because of the Covid pandemic, Alex and Sophie were forced to think about whether theatre making was possible in a digital arena. It seemed difficult to imagine how it might look because, as we have seen from the *Create, Play, Perform* workshops, the process involves working collaboratively towards an end result shown to a live audience. Nevertheless, restriction rules brought about a need for interacting with people in innovative ways, and one of these was an online learning project devised by Alex and Sophie called *Echoing*.

Collaborating online with sound designers, young people chose a location around the city of Bath to write a soundscape for. After taking part in live virtual workshops that introduced apps such as Audacity to facilitate producing sequences of sounds that hinted at various narratives (some including music, others dialogue), physical QR codes were posted in situ around Bath so that audiences armed with their own personal devices could '*follow the digital breadcrumbs to eavesdrop*'. The potential reach to audiences who might stumble upon the QR codes, intrigued by what they were, was a positive prospect for the project; possibly for some people opening up a theatre encounter for the first time.

It might even have led to people being inspired enough to create their own soundscapes, and in turn to share these with others who might do the same, therefore entering into a 'cycle of creativity' (Hosack Janes, 2014, p 100) as outlined in Chapter 3. However, what was unavoidably lost in the QR code *Echoing* project experience was a sense of simultaneous togetherness. Simon McBurney from Complicité talks about this as being critical to a theatrical event. Let us briefly look at what he says.

As previously mentioned in Chapter 1, Marcus du Sautoy was involved in bringing to the stage Complicité's production *The Encounter*, a show that explores theatre through the subject of consciousness. Simon McBurney, who directed the play, explains in a recorded conversation with Marcus du Sautoy (Complicité, 2018) why he finds the subject fascinating:

> What is consciousness? Is it a consequence of evolution and language, something that the brain has produced ... Is it just this thing in our heads?

Marcus du Sautoy agrees that theatre is an interesting place to explore these thoughts because:

> there is a sense that with an audience there's something more than just the individual consciousnesses of the audience members and the people on the stage. There's something else beginning to appear.

The Encounter is inspired by a true story about a photographer who found himself lost in the rainforest of the remote Javari Valley, in Brazil. In preparation for developing the play, based on the book *Amazon Beaming* by Petru Popescu, Simon McBurney retraced the journey of the photographer and met the indigenous people who live there: the Mayoruna. Before setting off, Simon researched around the subject of consciousness, asking actors, scientists and psychotherapists about what it means to be conscious and where they think it exists. He then asked the same question to the Mayoruna, who pointed at the forest. This was a different reaction, which until then had centred on things to do with the head. After some effort to ensure that he was not misunderstanding, he realised that the Mayoruna 'did not feel that their inner world was separate from the world around them'. Simon concluded that this is like what happens in the space between actors on a stage and the audience. 'Theatre', he says, 'only exists when the audience is there'. It is not that it is in the minds of the audience either, he explains, it exists in the communal space between them and the actors, and is the reason, he believes, why people go to the theatre. He says:

> They suddenly laugh together. They cry together. And they realise that this thing they have inside their heads is existing simultaneously in the minds of everyone else. In other words they cannot be, and are not, alone.

Theatre, therefore, explained in such a way, is a humanising experience, bearing the same qualities articulated by Dewey (1934) in his theory on aesthetics (see Chapter 3). To borrow Dewey's phrase, we might say 'drama as experience'. The communal theatre experience can also be explained in terms of Csikszentmihalyi's thoughts on 'social flow' (Csikszentmihalyi, 1997, p 70) (also see Chapter 3).

In a statement on the Complicité website (Autumn, 2021), Simon McBurney encapsulates the overall goal of the theatre company:

> *Complicité's vision – to create work that strengthens human interconnection, using the complicity between the performer and the audience that is at the heart of the theatrical experience – has never been more urgent at this time where violent division has become the norm.*

> *We live in a moment of unprecedented, sometimes brutal, and ever accelerating change. Pushing the limits of artistic experiment, which has always been key to the Company's vision, is a vital tool in unlocking the most urgent and crucial questions of our times, challenging, and excavating conventional accepted norms.*

In the following case study, the question over whether it is possible for an audience to enter into a simultaneous shared experience when not physically in the same space is tested somewhat by them watching a play together at the same time (even though it is recorded) and then being able to interact with others afterwards to share what they thought about what they had seen.

Though This Be Madness: a co-created play by the Mandala Theatre Company

An audience's acute awareness of a drama unfolding in front of them is pivotal to relaying the hard-hitting messages about issues surrounding knife crime in the Mandala Theatre Company production *Though This Be Madness*. The play was, before the pandemic, to tour the UK. However, although this was no longer possible due to Covid restrictions, because people were becoming more used to accessing live content online, when the play was first shown in 2021, performed in the intimate space of the Burton Taylor Studio managed by Oxford Playhouse, many more people than could fit in the theatre, or who could travel to see the play, were able to view it virtually during special events that were part recorded/ part live. These included Q&A sessions with the director, Yasmin Sidhwa.

Though This Be Madness examines what can happen to young people in relation to exclusion and gang grooming, and how too often this is a '*pipeline*' to prison (the working title of the play was *Pipeline*). The publicity flier for the production tells us that the play is an exploration of '*what lies behind the headlines*', and asks '*Can we change the story?*' The objective of producing the play, co-created with young people, some with lived experience of the themes, was to stimulate discussion. And this happened during live online interactions.

The play centres on the characters Tachia, Cass and Mickey who, all in their teens, have ended up outside of mainstream education. They attend a Pupil Referral Unit (PRU), and are taught by a very well-meaning, hardworking teacher called Mr Jones. However, it is not until he asks them for their responses to *Hamlet* does he interest them in their education. At first, Shakespeare's tale seems so far removed from his students' own life experiences that they do not immediately engage. But, the teacher tells them that Hamlet is '*an angry man, like you … He thinks he's going mad'*. Suddenly, they see the point and start to make connections with their own experiences.

Here, we see the teacher in the play employing an experiential model of learning, as characterised by Dewey (see Chapter 3). And it is the same model of learning that Yasmin and the writer, Avaes Mohammad, used to gather content material for the play. I interviewed Yasmin about how this worked in practice. She told me:

> The co-creation comes from spending a long time doing weekly sessions [this included four months of weekly sessions at two PRUs, plus one and two-day workshops in various locations across the UK]. I wouldn't go in and ask about their [the young people's] stories, of course. It was very much about creating a fictious story together.

> We actually started from the point of view of a newspaper article about a fictious young person going to a young offenders' institution and we tracked back to think about 'what has created this?' … We'd jump into what it might feel like … We did lots of role play … Some of the young people would really want to come and listen … Others would get up and do it and they would be brilliant at it … So, it [the play] came very much out of what they first fictitiously started to think about … Obviously they would reveal stuff about themselves which we did not directly use … It's no one person's story [the final play].

She went on to tell me about the next step in the process:

> The writer and I saw the young people react to the workshops and then that fed into our process where we discussed it all. And then he went away and wrote the first draft, which we then took back to the same young people. … We rehearsed the piece … Script in hand, but a lot of it the young people had learnt.

> We got their feedback … They engaged in discussions … We asked them what they liked about the story. How true it was? What they felt about the characters? Would there be anything they would want to change?

> The only thing really they wanted to change – they did feel one of the gang members was too angry. That really these gang leaders are so charismatic – so charming – that people are drawn to them … They are very clever manipulators, as we see in the play.

Yasmin was very clear that the play is:

> very much about feeling like you belong … and if there is no sense of belonging, you can start to belong somewhere else where you feel you're being listened to.

It is a very powerful message that not only relates to gang culture.

The creative learning opportunities offered to the young people involved in the development of both the *Create, Play, Perform* and *Though This Be Madness* plays include experiences where the arts are valued as essential in the process of communicating ideas. Experimental thinking and collaboration are also encouraged through role play and thinking around subjects that are relevant to the young people.

Greek Tragedy Masterclasses on Film

This third example of how drama can help to nurture personal creativity grew from a partnership between the theatre company Out of Chaos and the Centre for Hellenic Studies at Harvard University. Together they post monthly readings online of different Greek tragedies. The Greek Tragedy Masterclasses on Film project, also working in partnership with the Archive of Performances of Greek and Roman Drama (APGRD) at the University of Oxford, sees actors and academics interpreting key scenes from classical Greek texts in different ways, exploring the motivations of characters in online workshops.

In the same way that the foremost aim of the National Gallery, London, is to '*to establish a central role for Old Master paintings in modern cultural life*' (The National Gallery, 2017, p 2), as mentioned in Chapter 5 when we looked at the Take One Picture scheme, the overall objective for the work of Out of Chaos, as their website states, is to '*investigate old stories and their enduring relevance to modern audiences*'. They do this through including the audience '*within the action of the play by conferring power and agency on them*'. In the *Interpreting Antigone* (2021) workshop, Paul O'Mahony, the artistic director, explains how this is achieved.

He and two actors were in a room for two days just looking at one scene between Antigone and King Creon, thinking about the different ways the characters could be acted out. He says they found they were '*just scratching the surface at the different interpretations that there might be*'. The masterclass shows some of these explorations with the aim of demonstrating '*how interpretation shapes a production and how through rehearsal a performance gets built that can vary very differently from other interpretations you might see*'. In other words, the process of interpreting a play is a creative one. Audience agency comes about by encouraging individual responses from those who are watching the masterclasses, helping them make relevant connections to their own experiences ie using the experiential strategies that we discussed at the end of Part 2 and in Chapter 5 (Hosack Janes, 2021).

Evelyn Miller, the actor who plays Antigone, sees this ability to interpret as '*incredibly empowering, not only as an actor, but I would hope for someone watching, or studying, or just reading the text for enjoyment*'. She goes on to say:

> *I think there's something very powerful about understanding that each person who performs it [the character] will have a different take, even if they're aiming for the same thing. The very fact of their being – their body, their voice, their life experience – shifts the words and how they're received by an audience. I think it's the most magical thing.*

Because audience access is only through recorded content, as already considered in this chapter, a sense of togetherness, of potential humanising moments of '*social flow*'

(Csikszentmihalyi, 1997, p 70), is inevitably lost. However, this absence could be lessened by using the Greek Tragedy Masterclasses on Film workshops as a focus for discussion with others – either others in the same physical space, or virtually through live audience interaction (as with the *Though This Be Madness* special online events), or even taking ideas from the masterclass to produce something that is a uniquely personal response which could be shared with others in a *'cycle of creativity'* (Hosack Janes, 2014, p 100).

Sharing creative responses

The opportunity to share individual creative responses, online through creative challenges and through the use of social media and television programmes, has become very popular in recent years, particularly during the pandemic when some people had more spare time. When I was a child these opportunities existed, and I joined in with them – sending my poster designs and the like into *Blue Peter* and Tony Hart (ask someone over the age of 50 if you have not heard of him!), but there are many more chances to share your creativity now.

One of my favourite collective creative challenges is Kate Pullinger and Neil Bartlett's *Letter to an Unknown Soldier* project, described on the project website as *'a new kind of war memorial made by thousands of people'*. On the 100th anniversary of the declaration of the First World War, everyone in the UK was invited to write a letter to the unknown soldier commemorated in the statue on platform 1 of Paddington Station, London. These letters are a lasting tribute to those who died.

The challenge of curating your own exhibition on the Art UK website, the home for every public art collection in the UK, using their online 'curations' tool is really interesting too. As are the numerous drawing challenges that can be found online, such as Jake Parker's *Inktober* and Susan Yeate's *30-Day Sketchbook Challenge*. For both of these you are invited to upload your drawings if you would like to, but it is not necessary. I tend not to, but I enjoy the sense of knowing that lots of other people are grappling with the same quandary of which 'thing beginning with W' to draw. Creatively interpreting themes happens with photographic challenges too, for example, *The Guardian* newspaper runs their ongoing *In Pictures* challenge.

Over lockdown in the UK in 2020 *Grayson Perry's Art Club* was a huge success, with people sending in their artistic responses on a weekly theme. It was so enjoyable to see how many different ways one theme could be interpreted, and how genuinely encouraging Grayson Perry and his wife, Philipa Perry, and guests were for us all to just have a go! The *Great Big Art Exhibition* was another nationwide challenge to get involved in during the pandemic. And if you did not want to draw, paint or make a sculpture, there was always the Getty Museum challenge to recreate your favourite artwork with things lying around the house. That was great fun!

An Office of Standards in Education (Ofsted) special subject report in 2012 called Making a Mark: Art, Craft and Design Education 2008–11 stated that:

Teachers' subject expertise in drawing varies widely. In primary schools, teachers' lack of confidence in their own drawing abilities meant they were reluctant to demonstrate drawing techniques to pupils and to assess pupils' progress. In the secondary and post-16 sectors teachers were more skilled in drawing and had a good understanding of how to introduce students to approaches used by other creative practitioners. However, most viewed observational drawing as the principal vehicle for teaching drawing. As a result, relatively few schools used imaginative starting points for drawing, which narrowed opportunities for pupils to develop their skills through different approaches.

(Ofsted, 2012, p 62)

I would suggest that nurturing our own creativity through such group challenges like the ones I have just mentioned – perhaps regularly sketching for ten minutes a day, or taking photographs on your phone that illustrate a theme, or like Andrew Marr taking a '*grimy bag full of oil paints and a canvas*' up a mountain, or wherever takes your fancy – that this process of combining your own skills and imagination will help you to impart an enthusiasm for creativity to others, that in turn will help their own creativity to flourish.

REFLECTIVE POINTS

- Are there similar initiatives that you know about that aim to nurture creativity? What do they share with the examples given in this chapter? Perhaps you have experienced your own creativity being developed by a project?

- Take a look at some of the websites mentioned in this chapter that offer creative challenges and have a go at a creative challenge yourself!

References

Claxton, G (1998) *Hare Brain, Tortoise Mind: Why Intelligence Increases When You Think Less*. London: Fourth Estate.

Complicité (2018) Interview between Simon McBurnet and Marcus du Sautoy on The Encounter. [online] Available at: https://www.youtube.com/watch?v=HvHpYd5wZbA (accessed 10 August 2021).

Complicité website. [online] Available at: http://www.complicite.org/productions-home.php (accessed 1 September 2021).

Craft, A (2001) Little c Creativity, in Craft, A, Jeffrey, B and Liebling, M (eds) *Creativity in Education*. London: Continuum, pp 45–61.

Csikszentmihalyi, M (1997) Finding Flow. *Psychology Today*, 30, 4; Health Research Premium Collection.

Dewey, J (1934) *Art as Experience*. New York: The Berkley Publishing Group.

Dewey, J (1938) *Experience and Education*. New York: Touchstone (first Touchstone edition published 1997).

Hosack Janes, K (2014) *Using the Visual Arts for Cross-Curricular Teaching and Learning*. Abingdon: Routledge.

Hosack Janes, K (2021) Objects of Curiosity: How Old Master Paintings Have Been Used in the Primary Classroom to Provide Pupils with Cognitive Challenge and Creative Agency. *Thinking Skills and Creativity*, 41.

Inktober website. [online] Available at: https://inktober.com/ (accessed 3 September 2021).

Letter to an Unknown Soldier project website. [online] Available at: https://www.1418now.org.uk/letter/ (accessed 15 September 2021).

Mandala Theatre Company website. [online] Available at: https://www.mandalatheatre.co.uk/home (accessed 2 July 2021).

Marr, A (2013) *A Short Book about Drawing*. London: Quadrille Publishing Ltd.

Office of Standards in Education (Ofsted) (2012) Making a Mark: Art, Craft and Design Education 2008–11. [online] Available at: https://www.gov.uk/government/publications/art-craft-and-design-education-making-a-mark (accessed 12 September 2021).

Out of Chaos (2021) Greek Tragedy Masterclass: Interpreting Antigone. [online] Available at: https://www.youtube.com/watch?v=Y6Qi3RjODIk&t=10s (accessed 2 July 2021).

Out of Chaos website. [online] Available at: https://www.out-of-chaos.co.uk/ (accessed 2 July 2021).

Susan Yeate's 30-day Sketchbook Challenge website. [online] Available at: https://susanyeates.co.uk/pages/30-day-sketchbook-challenge (accessed 3 August 2021).

The National Gallery (2017) The National Gallery Annual Report and Accounts for the Year Ended 31 March 2017. [online] Available at: https://www.nationalgallery.org.uk/media/24777/annual-report-accounts_2016-17.pdf (accessed 12 March 2021).

Theatre Royal Bath website. [online] Available at: https://www.theatreroyal.org.uk/ (accessed 3 September 2021).

Vygotsky, L S (trans.) (1978) *Mind in Society: The Development of Higher Psychological Processes*, Cole, M, John-Steiner, S, Scribner, S and Souberman, E (eds and trans). Cambridge, MA: Harvard University Press.

Vygotsky, L S (trans.) (1987) *The Collected Works of L.S. Vygotsky. Vol 1: Problems of General Psychology* (including the volume *Thinking and Speech*), Rieber, R W and Carton, A S (eds), Minick, N. (trans). New York: Plenum Press.

Vygotsky, L S (trans.) (2004) Sharpe, M E (trans). *Imagination and Creativity in Childhood*. *Journal of Russian and East European Psychology*, 42 (1): 7–97.

Conclusion to Part 3

At the start of this book we talked about how defining creativity is tricky, but why it is important to try. The explorations we have taken together, I hope you agree, have in fact shown that there is a great deal of consensus across theory and practice; not only about what creativity looks like, but also how to go about creating the right conditions for it to be nurtured. Different words and phrases might be used to describe these, and thinking about the reasons for the differences in language is important because the nature of creativity is complex. But overall, the wide range of examples of theory and practice in this book have, I hope, helped you to find your own creative way of thinking about creativity in education.

To conclude, both as an educator and as a parent, I am left with the impression that if children and young people are able to be exposed to a wide range of art forms from different cultures across time and places, and if we welcome the richness that this variety brings, and if we put in place ample time for children and young people to play with their imaginations, as well as with their hands, and if we do this not just for the very young in their playgroups or on playdates, but for all children and young people – and indeed for (and with) adults too – then we will definitely be opening up opportunities for creativity to flourish. How could we not.

Also, let us not forget how creativity thrives on collaborative opportunities, and how these need to be made available to children and young people to readily take up. Some guided by adults, and some self-directed by those being creative themselves.

Ask yourself if an increase in any, or all, of these conditions would have made a difference to your own creative development when growing up, and if there are children you know that would benefit from such conditions now.

Index